Crossroads Café
WORKTEXT A

The publication of *Crossroads Café* was directed by the members of the Heinle & Heinle Secondary and Adult ESL Publishing Team.

Editorial Director:	Roseanne Mendoza
Senior Production Services Coordinator:	Lisa McLaughlin
Market Development Director:	Andy Martin

Also participating in the publication of the program were:

Vice President and Publisher, ESL:	Stanley Galek
Developmental Editor:	Nancy Mann Jordan
Senior Assistant Editor:	Sally Conover
Production Editor:	Maryellen Killeen
Manufacturing Coordinator:	Mary Beth Hennebury
Director of Global ELT Training and Development:	Evelyn Nelson
Full Service Design and Production:	PC&F, Inc.

Manufactured in the United States of America.

ISBN: 0-8384-66125

Heinle & Heinle is a division of International Thomson Publishing, Inc.

Photo Credits
Episodes 1, 2, 3, 4, 5, 6, 9, 10, 13, 14, 16, 17, 18: Stanley Newton
Episodes 7, 8, 11, 12, 15, 19, 20, 21, 22, 23, 24, 25, 26: Jane O'Neal

Crossroads Café
WORKTEXT A

K. Lynn Savage • Patricia Mooney Gonzalez • Mary McMullin
with Kathleen Santopietro Weddel

HEINLE & HEINLE PUBLISHERS
I T P *An International Thomson Publishing Company*
Boston, Massachusetts 02116 U.S.A.

*New York • London • Bonn • Boston • Detroit • Madrid • Melbourne • Mexico City • Paris •
Singapore • Tokyo • Toronto • Washington • Albany, NY • Belmont, CA • Cincinnati, OH*

Table of Contents and

	Title	Ways to Learn	Function/Structure*
1	Opening Day	Know Your Strengths	Giving and Getting Personal Information: *My name is . . .; I am from . . .*
2	Growing Pains	Identify Your Needs	Making Introductions: *I am . . .; This is . . .*
3	Worlds Apart	Set a Goal	Talking about Wants: *Want a . . .; want to . . .; don't want to . . .*
4	Who's the Boss?	Make a Plan	Making Apologies: *I'm sorry that . . .; I'm sorry for . . .*
5	Lost and Found	Use Resources	Telling Someone to Do Something: *Do this . . .; Please do this . . .*
6	Time Is Money	Organize	Making Suggestions: *Why don't you . . .; Maybe you should . . .; How about . . .?*
7	Fish Out of Water	Listen for Meaning	Describe Experiences: *Have learned . . .; has done . . .*
8	Family Matters	Correct Your Own Mistakes	Making Offers: *I'll . . .; Would you like me to . . .?*
9	Rush to Judgment	Guess	Describing People: *Is short . . .; has long hair . . .*
10	Let the Buyer Beware	Think about Learning	Giving Compliments: *You are charming. This food is delicious.*
11	No Vacancy	Ask for Help	Asking for Meaning: *What does that mean? What do you mean?*
12	Turning Points	Be Active	Talking about Possibilities: *Might want . . .; might leave . . .*
13	Trading Places	Observe Others	Talking about Ability: *Can . . .; know how to . . .*

*Crossroads Café is correlated to The New Grammar In Action series 1–3.
Please order The Heinle Grammar Correlation Booklet, ISBN 0-8384-9895-7.

Scope and Sequence

SCANS* AT-A-GLAN

Video Time (min: sec) Worktext	Crossroads Café Lesson Plans	**SCANS** Discussion Focus
1 Opening Day		
• 3:03–4:33 • 11:45–14:13 Text p. 13 • Text p. 12	• Applying for the café food server job • Culture Clip: Finding and Interviewing for Jobs • What Do You Think?	• Information: *evaluate data* • Systems: *understand social systems, monitor and correct performance* • Thinking: *think creatively* and *make decisions*
2 Growing Pains		
• 3:59–5:55 16:58–18:13 • Text p. 26	• Henry's working predicament • What Do You Think?	• Personal Qualities: *choose ethical courses of action* • Interpersonal: *negotiate*
3 Worlds Apart		
• 12:08–13:56 21:14–23:03 • Text p. 40	• Different cultures, different expectations • What Do You Think?	• Systems: *design* and *understand social systems* • Interpersonal: *work with people from culturally diverse backgrounds*
4 Who's the Boss?		
• 7:54–10:26 21:26–23:02 • Text p. 54	• Jamal's lesson about lying and integrity • What Do You Think?	• Personal Qualities: *believe in own self-worth, choose right thing to do* • Information: *acquire and evaluate*
• 14:39–16:18 Text p. 55	• Culture Clip: Career Changes	• Systems: *understand organizational systems* • Information: *analyze and communicate*
5 Lost and Found		
• 6:07–8:07 • 12:55–13:51	• Disruptive behavior in the workplace • A solution to disruptive behavior	• Human Resources: *evaluate performance, provide feedback* • Interpersonal Skills: *teach others new skills*
• 17:53–19:37 Text p. 69 • Text p. 68	• Culture Clip: Neighbors form groups to prevent crime • What Do You Think?	• Systems: *understand and operate effectively within systems* • Information: *interpret and communicate*
6 Time Is Money		
• 10:00–11:59 • Text pp. 80–81	• Recommendations about efficiency and organization in the workplace • Read and Write	• Information: *organize and maintain information* Systems: *monitor and correct performance* Thinking: *solve problems* • Information: *organize*
• 12:09–14:21 Text p. 83	• Culture Clip: Time is important in the U.S.	• Resources: *allocate time*
• 15:50–17:48 • Text p. 82	• Different opinions about money and people • What Do You Think?	• Information: *interpret and communicate* • Interpersonal: *communicate ideas to justify position*
7 Fish Out of Water		
• 11:44–13:39 • Text p. 96	• Different opinions about cultural pride • What Do You Think?	• Personal Qualities: *believe in own self-worth* • Interpersonal: *persuade and convince others*

*SCANS is an acronym for the Secretary's Commission on Achieving Necessary Skills (U.S. Department of Labor, 1991)

CE LESSON PLANS

Video Time (min: sec) Worktext	Crossroads Café Lesson Plans	SCANS Discussion Focus
8 Family Matters		
• 15:15–17:35 • 9:29–11:59 Text p. 111	• Single-parent challenges in working • Culture Clip: Single Parenting	• Thinking: *solve problems* • Interpersonal: *persuade and convince others*
9 Rush to Judgment		
• 4:14–5:54 • 21:26–23:12 • Text p. 124	• Police mistake Jamal for burglar • Brashov vouches for Jamal • What Do You Think?	• Systems: *understand organizational systems* • Information: *analyze and communicate* • Thinking: *draw conclusions*
• 6:24–8:48 Text p. 125	• Culture Clip: Roles of a Police Officer	• Information: *acquire and evaluate*
10 Let the Buyer Beware		
• 4:37–7:07 • 8:02–9:37 • Text p. 138	• New customer charms Brashov • Brashov falls for scam • What Do You Think?	• Thinking: *draw conclusions* • Information: *acquire, evaluate* • Information: *analyze and communicate*
• 17:58–19:59 Text p. 139	• Culture Clip: Consumer Scams	• Information: *acquire and evaluate, analyze and communicate* • Thinking: *draw conclusions*
11 No Vacancy		
• 5:09–6:22 8:25–10:19 • Text p. 152	• Recognizing discrimination • What Do You Think?	• Personal Qualities: *integrity* Interpersonal: *work with people of diverse backgrounds* • Information: *acquire and evaluate*
• 20:16–22:10 • 13:16–16:46 Text p. 153	• Documenting discrimination • Culture Clip: Discrimination	• Thinking: *recognize problem, create and complete a plan of action* • Information: *interpret and communicate*
12 Turning Points		
• 10:06–11:48 22:32–23:42 • Text p. 166	• Café vandalism foiled • What Do You Think?	• Thinking: *choose best alternative based on facts* Systems: *work within the system* • Information: *acquire and evaluate, analyze and communicate*
13 Trading Places		
• 9:42–11:14 • 17:58–19:40 • Text p. 180	• Café employees trade places • Difficulty of trading places • What Do You Think?	• Resources: *use facilities and materials* Systems: *develop alternative system, monitor and correct performance* • Thinking: *use efficient learning techniques* • Information: *analyze and communicate*
• 21:54–23:47 • 6:46–9:35 Text p. 181	• Resolving an argument • Culture Clip: The Roles Couples Choose	• Personal Qualities: *self esteem, self management* Interpersonal: *negotiate* • Thinking: *solve problems*

Acknowledgments

Rigorous review by members of the National Academic Council contributed to the initial design as well as the philosophical underpinnings of the products: Fiona Armstrong, Office of Adult and Continuing Education, New York City Board of Education; Janet Buongiorno, Adult Literacy Enhancement Center, Edison, New Jersey; Yvonne Cadiz, Adult and Community Education Program, Hillsborough County Public Schools, Florida; the late Jim Dodd, Bureau of Adult and Community Education, Department of Education, Florida; Chela Gonzalez, Metropolitan Adult Education Program, San Jose, California; Chip Harman, United States Information Agency, Washington, D.C.; Edwina Hoffman, Dade County Public Schools, Florida; Maggie Steinz, Illinois State Board of Education; Dennis Terdy, Adult Learning Resource Center, Des Plaines, Illinois; Inaam Mansour, Arlington Education and Employment Program, Arlington, Virginia; Fortune Valenty, Perth Amboy Public Schools, New Jersey; Kathleen Santopietro Weddel, Colorado Department of Education.

Collaboration among the Institute for Social Research at the University of Michigan, Interwest Applied Research in Portland, Oregon, and the National Center for Adult Literacy provided evaluation data that guided modification of student materials and development of teacher/tutor materials. Guiding and directing the evaluations were Jere Johnston, Dan Wagner, Regie Stites, and Evelyn Brzezinski. Participating pilot sites included the following: Alhambra School District, California; The Brooklyn Adult Learning Center, New York City Board of Education; Dade County Public Schools, Florida; Mt. Hood Community College, Portland, Oregon; Jewish Family Services, San Diego, California; Polish Welfare Association, Chicago, Illinois; One-Stop Immigration Center, Los Angeles, California; Even Start Program, Northside Independent School District, San Antonio, Texas; Margarita R. Huantes, Learning and Leadership Development Center, San Antonio, Texas; San Diego Community College District.

The collaboration with INTELECOM resulted in provocative stories, which provided meaningful contexts for the *Worktext's* activities. Thank you to Sarah for graciously providing whatever was needed and holding everything together during the most frenetic stages of the project; Peter and Glenn for providing entertaining and relevant story lines; Bob for keeping everyone properly focused; and Sally, for her leadership as well as her commitment and involvement in all aspects of the project.

Extensive experience of Heinle & Heinle and its staff in publishing language-learning materials ensured quality print materials. The authors wish to thank Nancy Mann, *Worktexts* editor, for her professionalism and expertise; Sally Conover, *Photo Stories* editor, for the dedication, patience, and attention to detail that the Photo Stories required; Lisa McLaughlin, production coordinator, for ensuring that the extremely tight production schedule was met without sacrificing quality; Maryellen Killeen, production editor, for her infinite patience and good humor in sorting through the hundreds of photos for the Photo Stories; Roseanne Mendoza, acquisitions editor, for her willingness to take the risks that the development of cutting edge products requires and for her commitment to fighting for the things she believes in.

Lynn would like to thank Roseanne at Heinle & Heinle for inviting her to participate in the project and for the good times working and growing together again; Jann for the fun times in the initial development and the from-the-heart comments in her ongoing review; Sally at INTELECOM for her accessibility day and night; and sister Gail, who listens well.

Pat would like to thank Roseanne at Heinle & Heinle for including her in this meaningful project and for her support during challenging times; Lynn for being a good listener, for patient assistance in seeing the "big picture" and for providing pep talks as needed; Sally and Nancy at Heinle & Heinle for their guidance and insightful comments, no matter how crazy the production schedule. Pat would also like to thank "Berry" and Diane for their support, understanding, and technical assistance throughout the duration of this project.

Mary would like to thank Kirk, Mom, Dad, Helen, Toula, and the rest of the family for keeping her focused on the important things. She is also grateful to Lilly and Tommy for the funny things they do.

To the Learner: About *Crossroads Café*

These pages explain what the *Crossroads Café* program is and how to use it. If you have problems understanding these explanations, ask someone to read and discuss them with you. If you start with a clear idea of how to use *Crossroads Café* correctly, your chances for success will be great.

Crossroads Café provides a unique method to learn English. The use of a television series and videos will help you improve your English. The *Crossroads Café* books are excellent tools for helping you use the television series or the videos to improve your listening, speaking, reading, and writing in English. The next section explains how each piece of the program can help you. It also answers some important questions about the series and how it should be used.

What Is *Crossroads Café?*

Crossroads Café is a course for studying English. The course teaches English as it entertains. It also helps you understand North American culture and use that understanding to live and work in the culture more successfully.

What Are the Parts of the Program?

There are three parts of the program for learners.
- The 26 television programs or the videos
- The two *Photo Stories* books
- The two *Worktexts*

You will use television programs or videos with the *Photo Stories,* the *Worktexts,* or both to learn English.

What Are the Television Programs?

The television programs are the most important part of the *Crossroads Café* program. There are 26 thirty-minute episodes that tell the story of a group of hard-working, determined people whose lives come together at a small neighborhood restaurant called Crossroads Café. Some of them are newcomers to the United States. Others have families that have been here for one or many generations. These people slowly create a successful neighborhood restaurant. During the 26 episodes, *Crossroads Café* tells of the successes and the failures, the joys and the sadness, and especially the learning experiences of the owner of the café, the people who work in it, their families, friends, acquaintances, neighbors, and the people they must cooperate with to be successful in their work and in their lives. The story is sometimes funny, sometimes sad, but always entertaining. The large picture above shows the six main characters in *Crossroads Café*. The smaller pictures around it show the characters in their lives outside the café.

These are the people you will learn about in *Crossroads Café*. You will be able to understand many of the problems they face and share many of their feelings. You will learn from their experiences—learn English and learn something about North American culture. You will also discover new ways to learn—which can be new paths to success for you in an English-speaking culture.

Most of each thirty-minute program deals with the story of the café and its six characters. But there are two other pieces in each episode that are especially good for people who want to learn English and understand North American culture. In every episode, there is a short section called "Word Play." "Word Play" always shows and explains some special way English is used in that episode. It combines cartoons, illustrations, and scenes from the episode to teach how to use English for a special purpose. For example, "Word Play" presents ways to ask for help, make suggestions, or, as this picture shows, make complaints.

The second special section that is part of every episode is the "Culture Clip." It helps you understand North American culture. You can agree or disagree with the behavior the "Culture Clip" shows, but this section will always help you think about your ideas on culture, in your own country and in your life today. This can help you understand and deal with cultural differences.

How Do I Use the Television Programs or Videos?

You can use the program if you are any of these types of learner. Here's how each type can best use the television programs or the videos.

1. **The Independent Learner.** You want to study the language on your own—possibly with the help of a tutor, a friend, a neighbor, or a family member. You may have seen an episode of *Crossroads Café* on television, or you may have heard about it from someone else—a friend or a family member. You may have seen ads for the program in a store or a library. You ordered the *Crossroads Café* program on your own because you wanted to learn English at home, by yourself or with someone else.

2. **The Distant Learner.** You study in a distance-learning program in a school. You may talk to or see your teacher once a week, once every two weeks, or once a month. But most of your study will be done alone, using the *Crossroads Café* materials. Your teacher may tell you to watch *Crossroads Café* one or more times each week and do the activities in the *Worktexts,* the *Photo Stories,* or both. When you meet with your teacher—and perhaps with other students too—you will talk about what you saw and learned. You may also do some activities from the *Teacher's Resource Book* with the other students and your teacher.

3. The Classroom Learner. You study in a regular class with a teacher in a school. You will use the *Crossroads Café* books—*Worktexts, Photo Stories,* or both—in your class. Your teacher will ask you to watch *Crossroads Café* programs and do some of the activities in your book at home. In class, you will work with other students to do more activities in the *Worktext* or the *Photo Stories* and other activities from the *Teacher's Resource Book.* Your teacher may also show important pieces of the episodes again in class and discuss them with the students.

How Do I Use the *Worktexts?*

Each of the two *Crossroads Café Worktexts* contains thirteen episodes—half the episodes in the complete series. Every *Worktext* lesson has the same parts, which you will use to practice and improve your English before and after you watch the television or video.

The *Worktexts* are carefully written to help learners at three different levels of English study—high beginning, low intermediate, and high intermediate. You can "grow" with the program by using the same *Worktexts* and videos over and over as you acquire more English. Here's how these multi-level *Worktexts* can work for you.

The different activities in each section of the books are marked with colored stars— one, two, or three stars for the three different levels of learners. Here are two possible ways to use the *Worktexts.*

1. If you are working alone, without a teacher, try to work through all three levels in the first unit to see which level suits you best. Be honest with yourself. If you check your answers and see that you've made mistakes at a certain level, it's best to choose the level below that one. If you have a teacher or a tutor, he or she will probably choose a level for you. After you know your level, always do the activities for that level, as well as the activities for the levels before it. For example, let's say you decide you are a two-star learner. In every section, you will do the one-star activity first and then the two-star activity. If you are a three-star learner, you will do the one-star and the two-star activities before you do the three-star activity. Don't skip the lower-level activities. They are the warm-up practice that can help you succeed when you reach your own level.

2. In each section, go as far as you can in the star system. For example, in the first activity in an episode, you may be able to do both the one-star and the two-star activities easily. However, you may not be able to complete the three-star activity. So, stop after the two-star activity and move on to the next section. In the second section, you may be able to all three levels of stars easily, or you may only be able to do the one-star activity. Always begin with the one-star activity and, if you succeed, then move on to the more advanced activities. If you have problems with an activity, get help right away from your teacher or tutor, or from someone whose English is better than yours.

Remember, if you are studying alone you can choose one of those two ways of working. If you have a teacher or a tutor, that person can help you decide how to work. But if you have problems with any activity, always try to get help immediately from your teacher, your tutor, or someone else who knows more English than you. That way, you can understand what to do and how to correct yourself.

How Can the *Worktext* Activities Help Me Learn?

The *Worktext* activities do three things:

1. They help you understand the story on the video.

2. They provide language practice.

3. They ask you to think about, talk about, and write about your ideas.

Understanding the Story: To help you understand the story, the *Worktext* has activities for you to do before and after you watch the episode.

Before you watch, you can do three things:

- Look at the big picture on the first page for the episode. Look at the title. Then try to guess what the story is about. Talk about your ideas with someone.
- Then look at the six pictures in the "Before You Watch" section. Talk about the pictures with someone. Do the exercises that go with the pictures. Check your answers by looking at the answer key in the back of the book.
- Finally, read the questions in the "Focus for Watching" section. If you do not understand some words, use your dictionary, or ask someone what the words mean.

After you watch the episode, turn to the "After You Watch" activities in your *Worktext*. In these activities, you will do two things:

- You will match key people from the story with the focus questions.
- You will answer questions about important parts of the story and then you will put those parts in order.

Practicing the Language helps you develop your English language skills. This section of the *Worktext* gives you special activities to do after you watch the television or video. These next three sections will help you improve your grammar, your reading, and your writing.

Your New Language presents grammar for a special purpose. For example, you will learn to use commands to tell someone to do something. Or you will learn to use *can* and *know how to* to talk about what you are able to do. Here is a good way to do these activities:

- Watch "Word Play" on the video again, if possible.
- Complete the "Your New Language" section of your *Worktext*.
- Check your answers. Use the "Answer Key" in the back of the *Worktexts*.
- Practice the conversations in "Your New Language" with someone.

In Your Community presents the kind of reading you find in your everyday life. Here is a good way to do these activities:

- Answer the questions about the reading.
- Check your answers. Use the "Answer Key" in the back of your *Worktext.*
- Look for the same kind of reading in the town or city where you live.
- Compare the reading you find with the one in the *Worktext.*

Read and Write presents something that a person in *Crossroads Café* wrote. It may be a letter, a note, a diary page, or a newspaper article. Here is a good way to do these activities:

- Answer the questions about the main ideas of the writing.
- Guess the meaning of the words in the vocabulary exercises.
- Use your experiences to write about something similar.
- Share your writing with someone.

Two sections of each *Worktext* unit have exercises that ask you to give your opinions about something that happened in the story. These sections are called "What Do You Think?" and "Culture Clip."

Here is a good way to work through the **What Do You Think?** activities:

- Think about things people in the story have done or opinions they have expressed.
- Share your ideas with someone.

Here is a good way to work through the **Culture Clip** activities:

- Watch the "Culture Clip" on the video again, if possible.
- Identify the main ideas from the "Culture Clip."
- Give your own opinion about a situation related to the "Culture Clip."

Check Your English is the last activity in each unit. It is a review of vocabulary, grammar, and reading. You can check your answers with the "Answer Key" in the back of your *Worktext.*

What Are the *Photo Stories?*

The *Crossroads Café Photo Stories* do these things:

- They help you understand the story before you watch the video.
- They ask you questions to help you understand parts of the story.
- They help you improve your vocabulary.
- They help you review after you watch.

The *Photo Stories* can help you if you know a little English or a lot of English:

- They can be special books for beginning learners of English. Learners study the pictures from the video. These pictures have the words from the story in them. This combination of words and photos makes learning English easy. If you speak Spanish, you may have read *fotonovelas*, or *telefotonovelas*. The *Photo Stories* look very much like those books, and they tell interesting stories, too.

- They are also for more advanced students of English. They can be an extra help for you if you are using the *Worktexts*. You can use the *Photo Story* to preview each television or video episode. First read the *Photo Story* and then do the exercises. Then, when you watch the episode, you will be prepared to understand what is happening and know what the characters will say.

This sample page shows how the *Photo Stories* tell the story of the video and help you read to find the meaning.

13 Trading Places _____ **211**

This sample page shows one type of activity you will do after you read the story.

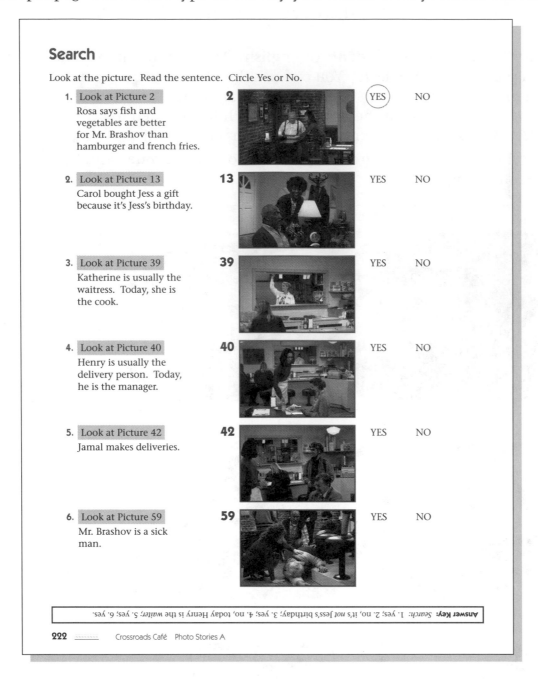

Special Questions about *Crossroads Café*

Learners of English and their teachers and tutors sometimes ask these questions about *Crossroads Café*.

What if I can't understand everything in the television or video episodes? Don't worry if you can't understand some language in the episodes. Even if you don't understand a lot of language, you can still learn from watching. You will often be able to guess what is happening in the story. This is because sometimes the people use actions that help you understand the meaning of their words. Also, sometimes they will look happy, surprised, or even angry when they speak. These facial expressions help you guess what they are saying. Learn to watch for these clues. They can help you understand the story. Good language learners know how to use these clues to help themselves. With *Crossroads Café*, you will learn to develop successful language-learning habits.

What if I can't understand the way some of the characters speak? In *Crossroads Café*, several important characters were either born in the U.S. or arrived when they were very young. They speak English without accents:

- Katherine is from the Midwest.
- Jess is from the South.
- Henry was born in China, but immigrated to the U.S. before he started school.

But some characters are from other parts of the world:

- Mr. Brashov is from Eastern Europe.
- Rosa was born in the U.S., but she grew up in Latin America.
- Jamal is from the Middle East.

These characters, like you, are still improving their English pronunciation, although they always use correct grammar. It will help you to hear many different pronunciations of English. In North America, and in the world in general, people speak English in many different ways. In schools, at work, and in the streets, other people need to understand them to communicate successfully with them. Becoming accustomed to hearing speakers from different cultures and different ethnic groups is a skill successful English speakers need to develop in our modern world.

What if the English is too fast for me? In *Crossroads Café*, the characters speak at a natural speed. Their speech is not artificially slow. In the real world, very few people talk slowly to help learners of English, so in *Crossroads Café* you will hear English spoken naturally. This will be helpful to you in the long run. But the *Crossroads Café* course can give you extra help as you become accustomed to hearing English at a normal pace. Here are four ways you can use the program to get this help:

- You can preview and review the story by using the *Photo Stories,* the *Worktext,* or both.
- If you meet with your teacher and your class, your teacher may use the video version to show again some important pieces of the episode you already watched.
- Your teacher may also show some pieces of a video episode *before* you see the complete episode at home on television.
- You can record complete episodes of *Crossroads Café* with a VCR and then play them back for yourself again and again. Or you may want to buy some or all of the video episodes by calling 1-800-ESL-BY-TV (1-800-375-2988) or 1-800-354-9706.

Why should I have a study partner? Learning a language means learning to communicate with others. Using videos and television programs to learn a language has many advantages, but seeing the programs and doing the reading, writing, and thinking activities in the *Worktext* is not enough. Having a study partner gives you the opportunity to practice your new language skills. That person can be another *Crossroads Café* English learner. It can be a wonderful shared experience to do the lessons and watch the videos with a partner who is also learning English. But your partner could also be someone who knows more English than you do. It can be someone who is not studying with the *Crossroads Café* materials—someone like a relative who knows English and can help you—perhaps a son or a daughter, a husband or a wife, or any other family member. Or the partner can be a neighbor, a person who works with you, a friend, or any person who knows more English than you do. And, finally, the partner can be a formal or informal tutor—a librarian, a high-school student, or someone who used to be a teacher. Any of these people can help make the time you spend learning English more productive. If your partner knows more English than you do, he or she can use the *Crossroads Café Partner Guide*. The *Partner Guide* is small and easy to use, but they have some excellent ideas for helping learners of English.

1 Opening Day

In this unit you will:

- get and give personal information
    - about names
    - about countries
- read job application forms
- write about people
- describe U.S. job interview behavior

Ways to Learn

Rosa and Maria tell Mr. Brashov about their skills for the job. Rosa and Maria know **what they do well**. They know their **strengths**. To **know your strengths** means to **know what you do well.**

Know Your Strengths

Check (✓) what you already **do well** in English.

- ☐ I understand most conversations.
- ☐ I use good English grammar.
- ☐ I speak with good pronunciation.
- ☐ I write clearly and correctly.
- ☐ I understand most of what I read.
- ☐ I use body language to show understanding.
- ☐ I want to learn and I am motivated.
- ☐ other: _____

On Your Own

Last week, what did you **do well** to learn English? Tell how and when you **used your strengths**.
For example: *On Tuesday, I had a conversation with my supervisor at work. He understood all that I said about the problems on the job.*

_____

_____

_____

Before You Watch

Look at the pictures. What do you see?

1.

2.

3.

4.

5.

6.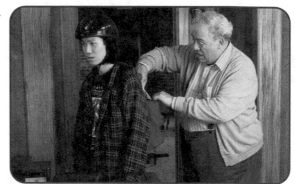

✪ What do you see in each picture? Write the number of the picture next to the word.

___3___ application form   ___4___ fire extinguisher

_____ backpack   _____ restaurant

___2___ chef   _____ tools

✪✪ What is happening? Write the number of the picture next to the sentence.

___5___ The handyman repairs something.

_____ The chef becomes angry and quits.

_____ The owner watches workers prepare his restaurant for opening day.

_____ The owner gives an application form to one of the applicants.

_____ The owner puts food in a teenager's backpack.

_____ Two people try to put out a fire.

✪✪✪ Write one question you have about each picture. Then read your questions to someone.

1. Who is the owner? _____

2. _____

3. _____

4. _____

5. _____

6. _____

Focus For Watching   Read the questions. Then watch.

✪ 1. Who is opening a restaurant?
2. Who is the new cook?
3. Who is the new waitress?

✪✪ 1. Who is the handyman?
2. Who delivers the food?

✪✪✪ 1. Who names the restaurant?

After You Watch

What do you remember? Match each question with the correct picture. You can use a picture more than once.

⭐ 1. Who is opening a restaurant?

a. Rosa

2. Who is the new cook?

b. Jamal

3. Who is the new waitress?

c. Mr. Brashov

⭐⭐ 1. Who is the handyman?

d. Katherine

2. Who delivers the food?

e. Jess

⭐⭐⭐ 1. Who names the restaurant?

f. Henry

✪ Read the sentence. Circle Yes or No.
1. The waitress quits.   YES   (NO)
2. The owner hires a waitress and a cook.   YES   NO
3. Katherine makes a delicious dessert.   YES   NO
4. Henry delivers the first order.   YES   NO

✪✪ Put the sentences in order. Number 1 to 4.

____ The chef quits.

_1_ Mr. Brashov is opening a restaurant.

____ He needs to hire a waitress, too.

____ He needs to hire a new chef.

✪✪✪ Write the story. Use the four sentences above. Add these three sentences. Then close the book and tell the story to someone.
- He hires Rosa because she makes a delicious dessert.
- He asks Jamal to fix the stove.
- There's a problem with the stove.

Mr. Brashov is opening a restaurant. There's a problem with the stove.

Your New Language: Giving and Getting Personal Information

To get personal information you can ask:
- What's your name?
- Where are you from?
- Where were you born?

To give personal information, you can say:
- My name is _____
- I am from _____
- I was born in _____

⭐ Complete the conversations. Use these words.

Jamal Al-Jibali	Victor Brashov	Egypt	Mexico
Rosa Rivera	Jess Washington	Mississippi	Romania

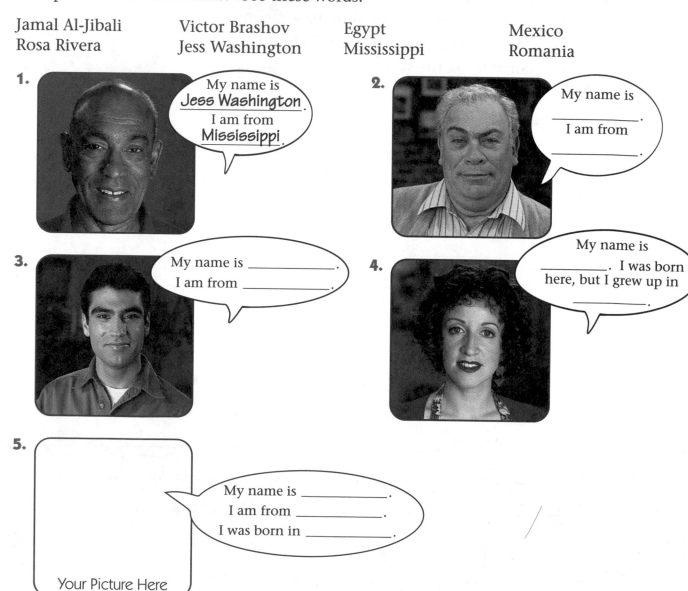

1.
My name is
Jess Washington.
I am from
Mississippi.

2.
My name is
_____.
I am from
_____.

3.
My name is _____.
I am from _____.

4.
My name is
_____. I was born
here, but I grew up in
_____.

5.
Your Picture Here

My name is _____.
I am from _____.
I was born in _____.

✪✪ Match.

1. What is his name?
2. Where is Jamal from?
3. What is Mr. Brashov's first name?
4. What is Katherine's last name?
5. Where was Rosa born?

a. His first name is Victor.
b. Her last name is Blake.
c. His name is Henry Chang.
d. She was born in Florida.
e. He is from Egypt.

✪✪✪ Complete the conversation. Use these words. Write one in each blank. You may use a word more than once.

am	you	from	is
he	was	his	

JESS: I am Jess Washington.

MR. BRASHOV: I _____am_____ Victor Brashov.
                        (1)

JESS: Are _____ from here?
                        (2)

MR. BRASHOV: No. I _____ born in Romania.
                        (3)

JESS: Who is that guy?

MR. BRASHOV: _____ is my handyman.
                        (4)

JESS: What is _____ name?
                        (5)

MR. BRASHOV: It _____ Jamal.
                        (6)

JESS: Is _____ from Romania, too?
                        (7)

MR. BRASHOV: No. He is _____ Egypt.
                        (8)

✪ Put the conversation in order. Number 1 to 4.

	HENRY:	Henry Chang.
	HENRY:	Yes?
1	MR. BRASHOV:	Excuse me, young man.
	MR. BRASHOV:	What is your name?

✪✪ Put the conversation in order. Number 1 to 5.

	ROSA:	I am Rosa Rivera.
	ROSA:	I am looking for Mr. Brashov.
	MR. BRASHOV:	Where are you from?
	MR. BRASHOV:	I am Mr. Brashov. Who are you?
	ROSA:	I was born in this country, but I grew up in Mexico.

✪✪✪ Put the conversation in order. Number 1 to 6.

	JESS:	I used to work for the post office. Now I'm retired.
	MR. BRASHOV:	Victor Brashov.
	MR. BRASHOV:	What do you do for a living, Jess?
	JESS:	Is that so?
	JESS:	The name is Jess. Jess Washington.
	MR. BRASHOV:	I used to be retired. Now I own this restaurant!

In Your Community: Job Applications

This is the job application that Katherine gave Mr. Brashov. Answer the questions about her application. Then tell your answers to someone.

APPLICATION FOR EMPLOYMENT		

Name: Blake / Katherine / Anne
Last / First / Middle

Address: 34 / Lincoln Ave. / 108
Number / Street / Apt.

Middletown / IL / 12345
City / State / Zip

Telephone: 217 / 555-4206
Area Code / Number

Social Security Number: 540-46-7951   U.S. Citizen ☑ yes   ☐ no

Employment Record	Present or Last Job	Previous Job
Job Position	waitress	waitress
Company Name	Mario's Restaurant	David's Sea Food
City	Middletown	Middletown
Dates of Employment	From 1/83 To 6/85	From 6/80 To 12/82
Job Duties: What did you do?	Present Job Waited on tables, prepared salads, set tables	Previous Job Head waitress at a 20-table restaurant

Person to be notified in case of emergency
Name: Lars Sorensen   Phone Number: (308) 555-1234
Address: PO Box 1956, Lincoln, Nebraska 68702

DATE: June 10, 1995   Signature: *Katherine Blake*

✪ 1. What is Katherine's middle name? _____

   2. What was her last job? _____

   3. When was her last job? _____

✪✪ 1. When was the last time Katherine had a job? _____

   2. How much experience does Katherine have? _____

✪✪✪ Do you think it would be easy for Katherine to get a job now? Why or why not?

I think/don't think it would be easy for Katherine to get a job now because _____

_____

Get a job application from an employer in your community. How is it the same as or different from this application?

Read and Write: Spotlight on Katherine

Katherine keeps a diary. A diary is a daily record about things you see and do. Read the questions. Read Katherine's diary entry quickly to find the answers. Circle the answers.

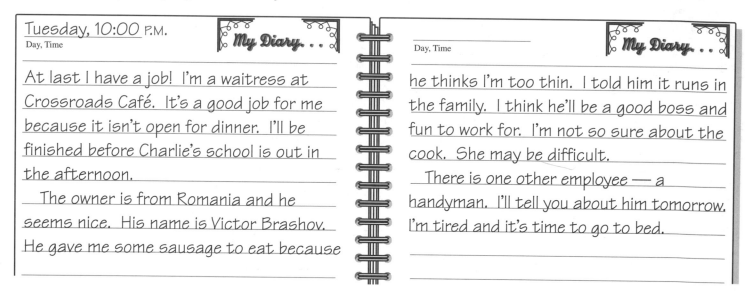

✪ What does Katherine write about?
   a. her son's school   b. her new job

✪✪ How does she feel about the job?
   a. unhappy and tired   b. happy but tired   c. happy and rested

✪✪✪ What is the tone or feeling of this diary entry?
   a. sad   b. cheerful   c. worried

Read the diary entry again carefully.

Tuesday, 10:00 P.M.
Day, Time

My Diary...

At last I have a job! I'm a waitress at Crossroads Café. It's a good job for me because it isn't open for dinner. I'll be finished before Charlie's school is out in the afternoon.

   The owner is from Romania and he seems nice. His name is Victor Brashov. He gave me some sausage to eat because

Day, Time

My Diary...

he thinks I'm too thin. I told him it runs in the family. I think he'll be a good boss and fun to work for. I'm not so sure about the cook. She may be difficult.

   There is one other employee — a handyman. I'll tell you about him tomorrow. I'm tired and it's time to go to bed.

Find the words in the reading. What do they mean? Circle the answer.

✪ **Boss:** someone who
   a. is nice   b. you work for   c. is fun

✪✪ **Employee:** someone who
   a. works at a place   b. is handy   c. you work for

✪✪✪ **Runs in the family**
   a. Katherine got sick
      from the sausage.
   b. Everyone in Katherine's family likes sausage.
   c. Other people in Katherine's family are thin, too.

Now you write an entry in a diary. In your entry, answer the following questions.

★   1. What is the the cook's name? Where is she from?

     2. What is the handyman's name? Where is he from?

     3. What is the name of the boy with the bicycle? Where is he from?

★★   1. Do you think the cook will be difficult to work with? Why or why not?

     2. Do you think the handyman will be fun to work with? Why or why not?

★★★   1. What is the name of the café?

     2. Who suggested the name? Why?

     3. If you could change the name, what would you name it? Why?

Read your entry to someone. Then ask: Did you understand? Do you have questions?

What Do You Think?

✪ Which person do you think will do the best job at Crossroads Café? Circle the name.

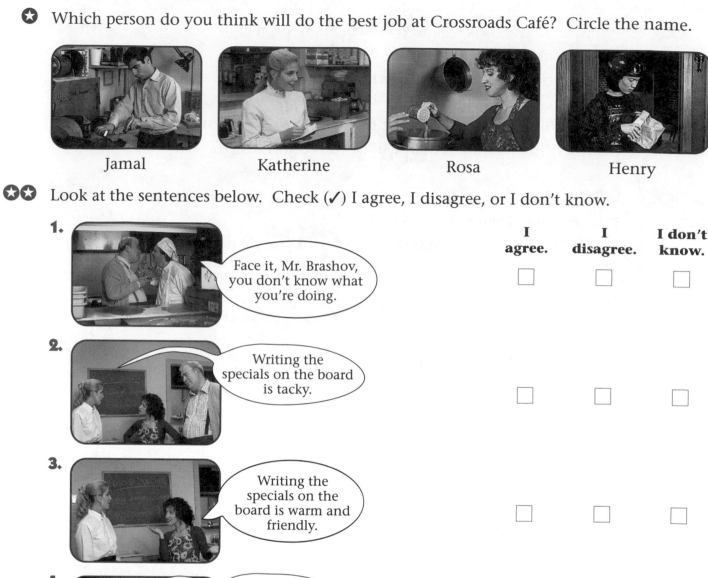

Jamal   Katherine   Rosa   Henry

✪✪ Look at the sentences below. Check (✓) I agree, I disagree, or I don't know.

	I agree.	I disagree.	I don't know.
1. Face it, Mr. Brashov, you don't know what you're doing.	☐	☐	☐
2. Writing the specials on the board is tacky.	☐	☐	☐
3. Writing the specials on the board is warm and friendly.	☐	☐	☐
4. Jamal doesn't look very handy to me.	☐	☐	☐

✪✪✪ Answer the questions. Then read your answers to someone.

1. Do you think Mr. Brashov's restaurant will be successful? Tell why or why not.

_____

2. Do you think Rosa and Katherine will become friends? Tell why or why not.

_____

3. Do you think Jamal is very handy? Tell why or why not.

_____

Culture Clip: Finding Jobs and Interviewing for Jobs

✪ Match the ways to find out about jobs.

1. Call the personnel office of a company.

2. Look in the classified ads.

3. Go to an employment agency.

a.

b.

c.

✪✪ Complete the rules for a good job interview. Write one word in each blank. Use these words.

alert	eye contact	job	rules
confident	handshake	questions	

Here are some general ___rules___ to follow in a _____ interview.
                       (1)   (2)

- Dress in conservative colors — blues, grays, blacks, white.

- Give a firm _____. It says you are awake, you are _____ and
                 (3)   (4)
  ready for a good day's work.

- Answer _____ with information that tells what you can do and what
             (5)
  you know how to do well.

- Make good _____. It communicates sincerity and a sense of being
               (6)
  self-assured and _____.
                 (7)

✪✪✪ Before Mr. Brashov hired Katherine, he interviewed several applicants. Do you think they followed the rules for a good interview? Why or why not? Write your ideas. Then tell your ideas to someone.

_____

_____

_____

Check Your English

✪ Write the correct word under each picture.

chef
application
    form
tools
fire extinguisher
restaurant
backpack

1. _____ 2. _chef_ 3. _____ 4. _____ 5. _____ 6. _____

✪✪ Make a sentence or question from each group of words.

1. name   first   Mr. Brashov's   is   Victor

   <u>Mr. Brashov's first name is Victor.</u> OR <u>Is Mr. Brashov's first name Victor?</u>

2. Rosa   from   where   is

_____

3. is   Henry   China   from

_____

4. what   name   Katherine's   is   last

_____

✪✪✪ Finish the story. Use the words in the box. Write one word in each blank.

Victor Brashov is the __owner__ of a new restaurant. He has many
                    (1)
things to do. There are _____ with the stove and the refrigerator. His
                         (2)
_____ quits. He needs to hire a _____ or waitress. There are
(3)   (4)
several applicants, but he doesn't like them. He needs a _____ for
                                  (5)
his restaurant.

Katherine applies for the _____ opening. She is different from the
                     (6)
others. Brashov _____ her. He hires another waitress _____,
         (7)   (8)
Rosa, to be his cook. His _____, Jamal, fixes the stove and the
                (9)
_____. Henry Chang, a teenager with a bicycle, comes into the
(10)
restaurant to ask _____ to the post office. Henry makes the first
                (11)
_____ for the restaurant. Jess, the first customer, names the
(12)
restaurant.

applicant
chef
cook
delivery
directions
fires
freezer
handyman
hires
name
owner
problems
stove
things
waiter
waitress

2 Growing Pains

In this unit you will:

- introduce yourself and others
- read school-related forms
- rewrite a newpaper article
- describe immigrant families in a new culture

Ways to Learn

Henry says *he needs* to work at Crossroads Café to earn money to buy a guitar. Henry's parents think *he needs* to spend his time studying.

Identify Your Needs

When do you *need* English?
Fill in the blank with 1, 2, or 3.

   1 = often   2 = sometimes   3 = never

___ to talk to my family and friends
___ to understand and talk to my doctor
___ to fill out forms or applications
___ to talk to and understand my supervisor at work
___ to read letters, newspapers, or work materials
   to talk to my children's teachers
___ to shop or bank
___ to talk to my teacher at school
___ other: _____

On Your Own

When and where did you *need* English last week?

When	Where

Before You Watch

Look at the pictures. What do you see?

1.

2.

3.

4.

5.

6.

✪ What do you see in each picture? Write the number of the picture next to the word.

__5__ work-study form   _____ birthday cake

_____ parents   _____ customer

_____ violin   _____ health and safety inspector

✪✪ What is happening? Write the number of the picture next to the sentence.

_____ The woman is holding a violin case. She looks angry.

_____ Mr. Brashov is shaking hands with a man.

_____ Mr. Brashov and Henry are talking with a customer.

__1__ Mr. Brashov is talking to a woman who has some papers in her hand.

_____ Someone in Henry's family is having a birthday party.

_____ Henry and Mr. Brashov are in the office with Henry's parents.

✪✪✪ Write one question you have about each picture. Then read your questions to someone.

1. What is this woman doing? _____

2. _____

3. _____

4. _____

5. _____

6. _____

Focus For Watching   Read the questions. Then watch.

✪ 1. Who has a birthday party?
2. Who is on a work-study program?
3. Who is surprised to see Henry at Crossroads Café?

✪✪ 1. Who is angry to hear that Henry has a job?
2. Who helps Ms. Reilly with her inspection?
3. Who falls and hurts her knee?

✪✪✪ 1. Who suggests that Henry prove he can work, study, and practice the violin?
2. Who tells Henry that he must tell the truth to Mr. Brashov and his parents?

After You Watch

What do you remember? Match each question with the correct picture. You can use a picture more than once.

⭐ 1. Who has a birthday party?

2. Who is on a work-study program?

3. Who is surprised to see Henry at Crossroads Café?

⭐⭐ 1. Who is angry to hear that Henry has a job?

2. Who helps Ms. Reilly with her inspection?

3. Who falls and hurts her knee?

⭐⭐⭐ 1. Who suggests that Henry prove he can work, study, and practice the violin?

2. Who tells Henry that he must tell Mr. Brashov and his parents?

a. Mr. Brashov

b. Henry

c. Rosa

d. Ms. Reilly

e. Jamal

f. Mr. and Mrs. Chang

g. Edward

h. Uncle Fred

✪ Read the sentences. Circle Yes or No.

1. Ms. Reilly is Mr. Brashov's friend.   YES   (NO)
2. Henry goes to school in the morning and works in the afternoon.   YES   NO
3. Uncle Fred tells Henry's parents about the job.   YES   NO
4. Henry's parents are happy about the job.   YES   NO
5. Henry cannot work at Crossroads Café.   YES   NO

✪✪ Put the sentences in order. Number 1 to 6.

_____ At first, they tell Henry that he cannot work. When they see Henry's violin they change their minds.

_____ Henry is upset to see his uncle because he has not told his family that he works at Crossroads Café.

_____ Henry's Uncle Fred stops by for some pie and is surprised to see Henry.

_____ She is not the only unexpected visitor.

_____ When his parents discover that Henry is working, they are very angry.

__1__ One afternoon, the health and safety inspector arrives unexpectedly to inspect Crossroads Café.

✪✪✪ Write the story. Use the six sentences above. Add these four sentences. Then close the book and tell the story to someone.

• They decide that Henry must prove that he can work at Crossroads Café and keep up with his school work and violin lessons.
• She is there to make sure that the café has no health and safety violations.
• In fact, he has lied to Mr. Brashov and signed his father's name on the work-study form.
• Henry is surprised too.

One afternoon, the health and safety inspector arrives unexpectedly to inspect

Crossroads Café.

_____

_____

_____

_____

_____

_____

_____

Your New Language: Making Introductions

To introduce yourself you can say:

• **I am** *Victor Brashov* or **I'm** *Victor Brashov.*

To introduce someone else you can say:

• *Uncle Fred,* **this is** *Mr. Brashov,* the owner of the café. *Mr. Brashov,* **this is** my Uncle, Fred.

To respond to an introduction, say:

• **It's a pleasure to meet you.**

• **It's nice to meet you.**

• **Glad to meet you.**

✪ Complete the conversations. Use these words.

too   the health inspector   Henry's mother   the owner
Henry's uncle

1.

2.

3.

4.

✪✪ Match.

1. This is my mom and dad, Mr. and Mrs. Chang.

2. It's a pleasure to meet you.

3. It's nice to meet you.

4. This is my uncle, Fred.

5. I'm Katherine, the waitress at Crossroads Café.

a. It's a pleasure to meet you.

b. Hi, I'm Victor Brashov, Henry's employer.

c. It's a pleasure to meet you, too.

d. We're Henry's parents, Mr. and Mrs. Chang.

e. It's nice to meet you, too.

✪✪✪ Complete the conversation. Use these words, phrases, or sentences. Write one in each blank.

this is	It's nice to meet you
the cook	Glad to meet you, too.
Glad to meet you	I'm
I'm Victor Brashov	It's a pleasure to meet both of you
the handyman	

MS. REILLY: _____I'm_____ Ms. Reilly, the health and safety
                              (1)
inspector.

MR. BRASHOV: _____. Welcome to Crossroads Café.
                              (2)
_____, the owner.
              (3)

ROSA: And I'm Rosa Rivera, _____.
                                              (4)

MS. REILLY: _____.
                    (5)

MR. BRASHOV: Ms. Reilly, _____ Katherine, our waitress
                                        (6)
and this is Jamal, _____.
                              (7)

JAMAL AND KATHERINE: _____.
                                    (8)

MS. REILLY: _____.
                    (9)

✪ Put the conversation in order. Number 1 to 4.

     ___   ROSA: Oh, nice to meet you. I'm Rosa, the cook.

     _1_   UNCLE FRED: Hi, I'm Henry's uncle, Fred.

     ___   ROSA: Yes. I'll get him.

     ___   UNCLE FRED: Nice to meet you, too. Is Henry here?

✪✪ Put the conversation in order. Number 1 to 5.

     ___   JESS: It's a pleasure to meet you. Henry's such a great boy.

     ___   JESS: Fine, Henry. How are things with you?

     ___   HENRY: Hi, Jess, how are you?

     ___   HENRY: O.K. Jess, this is my Mom and Dad, Mr. and Mrs. Chang. Mom and Dad, this is Jess.

     ___   CHANGS: Thank you. It's a pleasure to meet you also.

✪✪✪ Put the conversation in order. Number 1 to 6.

     ___   YOU: Not bad, thanks. Rosa, this is Bill Jones, my neighbor. Rosa Rivera, this is Bill Jones.

     ___   YOU: Hi, Rosa. How are you?

     ___   B: Nice to meet you.

     ___   A: Fine, thanks. How are you?

     ___   C: Nice to meet you too, Rosa.

     ___   YOU: Bill, Rosa is a great cook. You should try her special today.

In Your Community: Work-Study Permission Forms

This is the form that Henry needed for the work-study program. Answer the questions about the form.

Middletown High School
Middletown, IL
Work-Study Permission Form

I, _____Qi-min Chang_____ give permission to my (son)/daughter to participate in

the work-study program for _Spring Semester_, 19_96_.

I understand that (he)/she will attend regular classes in the _morning_ and

work in the _afternoon_. _Henry_ will be allowed to work

no more than _3 hours_ per day, and will not work more than _15 hours_ per

week. _Henry_ will be employed by_Crossroads Café_.

Henry Chang   _Qi-min Chang_
Student's Signature   Parent's Signature

Bob Smith   _Victor Brashou_
Counselor's Signature   Work-site Supervisor's Signature

★ 1. Can Henry work in the morning? _____

2. Can Henry work from 1:00 P.M. to 5:00 P.M. Monday through Saturday?

_____

★★ 1. Can Henry work from September to December? _____

2. Can Henry work at McDonald's? _____

★★★ 1. Do you think this form should be necessary? Why or why not?

_____

2. If you answered yes, do you think all four signatures should be necessary? Why or why not?

_____

Get forms that children bring home from schools in your community. How are they the same as or different from Henry's work-study permission forms?

Read and Write: Spotlight on Henry

Read the questions. Read Henry's article from his school newspaper quickly to find the answers. Then circle the answers.

✪ 1. What does Henry write about?
 a. his parents
 b. the work-study program
 c. his problems at Crossroads Café

✪✪ 2. Why does Henry write this article?
 a. to apologize to his parents
 b. to tell people about his great job
 c. to tell other students about the work-study program

✪✪✪ 3. What is the tone or feeling of the letter?
 a. bored
 b. apologetic
 c. enthusiastic

Read Henry's newspaper article again carefully.

MIDDLETOWN HIGH

WEDNESDAY
NOVEMBER 6, 1996
REPORTER
MIDDLETOWN HIGH SC
STUDENT NEWSPAPER

The Work-Study Program
by Henry Chang

There's a program at our school that's really great. It's the work-study program. It's great because you can go to school in the morning and work in the afternoon.

I really like it because I can finish high school and earn some money at the same time. That way, I don't have to ask my parents for everything. I can buy my own things. I also like it because I work at a great place – Crossroads Café. The people are really nice and interesting. We're a team, and I like that!

If you want to be a part of the work-study program, you need to get permission from your parents and the school. This is very, very important, believe me! You can pick up the permission form from the school office.

The work-study program is a great opportunity.

Find the words in the reading. What do they mean? Circle the answer.

✪ **great**
 a. excellent   b. O.K.   c. good

✪✪ **earn**
 a. ask for money   b. work for money   c. give money

✪✪✪ **permission**
 a. money   b. approval   c. assistance

Now you write an article for the newspaper. In your article answer the following questions.

⭐ Tell more about Henry. What kind of job does he have? What hours does he work?

⭐⭐ Tell more about the work-study program. How does a student get permission to work? Who must sign the form? Can a student work without the work-study form?

⭐⭐⭐ Tell more about Henry's problem. Why didn't he tell his parents? Why didn't he tell Mr. Brashov? Why did he sign the form? What happened when his parents found out?

Read your article to someone. Then ask: Did you understand? Do you have questions?

What Do You Think?

✪ Henry did not tell his parents about the job. Why? Check the reasons.

☐ His parents are Chinese, not American. They don't understand.

☐ He can do what he wants. He is not a child.

☐ It was not important.

☐ Other: _____

✪✪ Look at the sentences below. Check (✓) I agree, I disagree, or I don't know.

1.

	I agree.	I disagree.	I don't know.
	☐	☐	☐

Of course, I didn't lie. I just didn't mention that I work here. They think I'm in school every day until 3 o'clock.

2.

	☐	☐	☐

You lied not only to your parents, but to me . . . to all of us.

✪✪✪ Answer the questions. Then read your sentences to someone.

1. Do you think Henry lied? Tell why or why not.

_____

2. Do you think Henry should have told his parents about his job?
Tell why or why not.

_____

Culture Clip: Family Traditions

★ Match.

1. Many parents leave
their countries for better
lives for their children.

a.

2. Children adapt better
and more quickly to
their new countries.

b.

3. Family traditions are
very important.

c.

★★ Complete the sentences. Write one word in each blank. Use these words.

richness	age	family	balance
independent	children	decisions	

We see that ___children___ are very _____ here, even at a very young
(1)   (2)

_____. It's great and we like it, but there are some _____ that must be made
(3)   (4)

at the _____ table. It is a delicate _____ blending old and new traditions.
(5)   (6)

But the result can add a _____ to the lives of the people involved.
(7)

★★★ Henry tells his parents that he wants to work because he doesn't want to
depend on them for everything. Do you think it's important for children
to be independent? Why or why not? Write your ideas. Then tell your ideas
to someone.

_____

_____

_____

_____

_____

Check Your English

✪ Write the correct word under each picture.

work-study
form

customer

parents

health and safety
inspector

violin

birthday cake

1.
health and safety
inspector

2.
_____

3.
_____

4.
_____

5.
_____

6.
_____

✪✪ Make a sentence from each group of words.

1. Ms. Reilly   Jamal   the   inspector   is   this   health

   Jamal, this is Ms. Reilly, the health inspector. _____

2. meet   nice   it's   you   to

   _____

3. to   too   you   meet   nice

   _____

4. Ms.   is   our   Reilly   handyman   Jamal   this

   _____

✪✪✪ Finish the story. Use the words in the box. Write one word in each blank.

There are several surprises at Crossroads Café. A health and safety

__inspector__ arrives unexpectedly to inspect Crossroads Café. She is not the
  (1)

only unexpected _____. Henry's Uncle Fred also comes one day and is
                   (2)

_____ to find Henry working there. Henry has not told his family
   (3)

about the _____ or about the work-study _____. When his
             (4)   (5)

_____ find out, they are very _____. Henry has put his father's
   (6)   (7)

_____ on the permission _____. At first, Henry's parents refuse
   (8)   (9)

to let him work. Then they agree that if Henry can _____ he can study
                                                        (10)

and practice his violin, he can continue to work at the café.

angry
form
happy
inspector
job
parents
program
prove
signature
surprised
visitor
work

3 Worlds Apart

In this unit you will:

- talk about things you want or want to do
- read the Yellow Pages of a telephone directory
- write a letter
- describe U.S. immigration

Ways to Learn

Rosa's *goal* is to stay in the United States and experience a new lifestyle. She *wants* to try a different life. A *goal* is an objective or purpose.

Set a Goal

Why do you want to learn English? Check (✓) your *goals* for learning English.

- [ ] to help my children and family
- [ ] to get a job or a better job
- [ ] to continue my education
- [ ] to do well in my business
- [ ] to know my community better
- [ ] to improve my health
- [ ] to get to know new friends and neighbors
- [ ] other: _____

On Your Own

Last week I worked on this *goal*. I _____
_____

It was difficult because _____
_____

I was successful because _____
_____

What helped you meet your *goal?* _____
_____

Before You Watch

Look at the pictures. What do you see?

1.

2.

3.

4.

5.

6.

✪ What do you see in each picture? Write the number of the picture next to the word.

__4__ flowers   _____ necklace

_____ pillow   _____ plan

_____ roommate   _____ suitcase

✪✪ What is happening? Write the number of the picture next to the sentence.

_____ The man brings Rosa flowers.

_____ Mr. Brashov receives a package.

_____ Rosa shows her plans to the man.

_____ A man comes to visit.

_____ The man gives Rosa a necklace.

_____ Rosa introduces the man to her roommate.

✪✪✪ Write one question you have about each picture. Then read your questions to someone.

1. _Who is the man with the flowers?_ _____

2. _____

3. _____

4. _____

5. _____

6. _____

Focus For Watching   Read the questions. Then watch.

✪ 1. Who wants to marry Rosa?
2. Who wants to open a restaurant?
3. Who lives with Rosa?

✪✪ 1. Who makes reservations for a lunch meeting?
2. Who receives a package from home?

✪✪✪ 1. Who has to leave work because of an emergency?
2. Who forgets to tell someone about the lunch reservation?

After You Watch

What do you remember? Match each question with the correct picture. You can use a picture more than once.

★ 1. Who wants to marry Rosa?

2. Who wants to open a restaurant?

3. Who lives with Rosa?

★★ 1. Who makes reservations for a lunch meeting?

2. Who receives a package from home?

★★★ 1. Who has to leave work because of an emergency?

2. Who forgets to tell someone about the lunch reservation?

a. Carrie

b. Rosa

c. Mr. Brashov

d. Miguel

e. Mrs. Gilroy

f. Katherine

✪ Read these sentences. Circle Yes or No.
1. Miguel wants Rosa to move to Mexico.   (YES)   NO
2. Rosa wants Miguel to stay in the U.S.   YES   NO
3. Rosa marries Miguel.   YES   NO
4. Rosa opens her own restaurant.   YES   NO

✪✪ Put the sentences in order. Number 1 to 4.

_____   Rosa decides not to go back to Mexico.

_1_   Miguel comes to visit Rosa.

_____   Miguel asks Rosa to marry him.

_____   Rosa shows Miguel her plans for a restaurant.

✪✪✪ Write the story. Use the four sentences above. Add these three sentences.
Then close the book and tell the story to someone.
- Miguel doesn't think Rosa's restaurant will be a success in Puebla.
- Miguel brings Rosa a present from home.
- Rosa makes plans for a restaurant in Puebla.

Miguel comes to visit Rosa. Miguel brings Rosa a present from home.

_____

_____

_____

_____

_____

_____

_____

_____

_____

_____

_____

Your New Language: Talking about Wants

To ask about wants, say:
- What do you want?
- What do you want to do?

To tell about wants, say
- I want *chicken*.
- I want *to eat*.
- I don't want *chicken*.
- I don't want *to eat*.

⭐ Complete these conversations. Use these words.

something to drink   to marry you   an international   to surprise me
menu

1.

2.

3.

4.

✪✪ Match.

1. Why does Henry want to leave work early?
2. Why does Nicolae send Mr. Brashov a pillow?
3. What do you want for dinner?
4. I want to make reservations for lunch tomorrow
5. Where do you want to go for dinner?

a. He wants to help Mr. Brashov sleep.
b. How about a hamburger and french fries?
c. He wants to go to a rock concert.
d. Let's go to that new restaurant.
e. For how many people?

✪✪✪ Complete the conversation. Use these words and phrases. Write one in each blank. You may use a word or phrase more than once.

want   want to
don't want   don't want to

MIGUEL: Rosa, I ____want to____ marry you.
                        (1)

ROSA: But we've been apart for more than a year.

MIGUEL: That's why I _____ us to marry.
                                (2)

           I _____ us to be apart.
                (3)

ROSA: There are still many things I _____ do.
                                              (4)

MIGUEL: We don't have to get married right away.

ROSA: Miguel, I _____ open my own restaurant.
                          (5)

           I _____ it in this country.
                (6)

MIGUEL: Rosa, I _____ you to come home.
                      (7)

ROSA: But I _____ give up what I have here.
                    (8)

✪ Put the conversation in order. Number 1 to 3.

____ MRS. GILROY: We want two orders of Monterey Chicken.

_1_ KATHERINE: Yes, Mrs. Gilroy. Can I help you?

____ KATHERINE: Do you want something to drink?

✪✪ Put the conversation in order. Number 1 to 5.

____ CARRIE: What do you want to do? Get married or open a restaurant?

____ ROSA: I don't know. He wants to help me open a restaurant in Puebla.

____ ROSA: I don't know.

____ ROSA: Miguel wants me to marry him.

____ CARRIE: That's great. Isn't it?

✪✪✪ Put the conversation in order. Number 1 to 6.

____ MIGUEL: Rosa . . . this is wonderful. The name is "Around the World?"

____ ROSA: Did you see the way I want to arrange things? I want to have the kitchen in the same room as the customers.

____ ROSA: Here. Let me show you my plans for a restaurant in Puebla.

____ MIGUEL: I'm not sure an international restaurant would be a success in Puebla.

____ ROSA: Yes. I want to serve great dishes from around the world. These are some menu ideas.

____ MIGUEL: Wait a minute, Rosa. People don't want to watch the food being cooked.

In Your Community: Telephone Directories

This page is from the Yellow Pages. The Yellow Pages list businesses. They may be in the back of a telephone directory or a separate telephone directory. Rosa looked here to find a school for a business class. Answer the questions about the schools. Then tell your answers to someone.

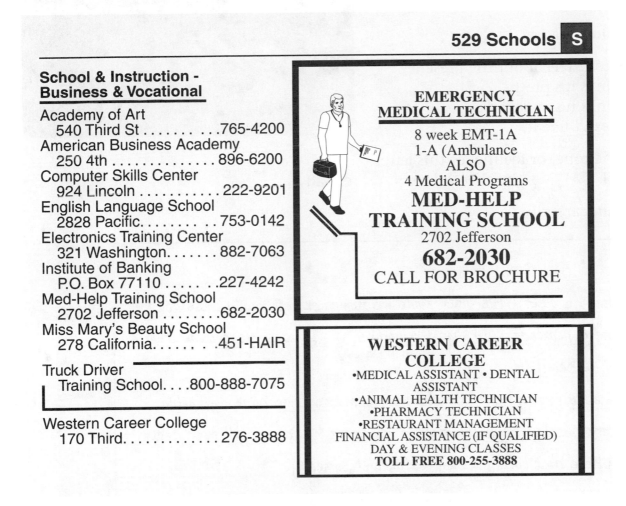

529 Schools **S**

School & Instruction - Business & Vocational

Academy of Art
540 Third St 765-4200
American Business Academy
250 4th 896-6200
Computer Skills Center
924 Lincoln 222-9201
English Language School
2828 Pacific. 753-0142
Electronics Training Center
321 Washington. 882-7063
Institute of Banking
P.O. Box 77110 227-4242
Med-Help Training School
2702 Jefferson 682-2030
Miss Mary's Beauty School
278 California. 451-HAIR

Truck Driver
Training School. . . .800-888-7075

Western Career College
170 Third. 276-3888

EMERGENCY MEDICAL TECHNICIAN

8 week EMT-1A
1-A (Ambulance
ALSO
4 Medical Programs
MED-HELP TRAINING SCHOOL
2702 Jefferson
682-2030
CALL FOR BROCHURE

WESTERN CAREER COLLEGE
•MEDICAL ASSISTANT • DENTAL ASSISTANT
•ANIMAL HEALTH TECHNICIAN
•PHARMACY TECHNICIAN
•RESTAURANT MANAGEMENT
FINANCIAL ASSISTANCE (IF QUALIFIED)
DAY & EVENING CLASSES
TOLL FREE 800-255-3888

✪ 1. What is the telephone number of the English Language School? _____

2. What is the address of Miss Mary's Beauty School? _____

3. Where is the Computer Skills Center? _____

✪✪ 1. Which schools have an 800 number?

2. What kind of restaurant training does the Western Career College offer?

✪✪✪ 1. Which school do you think Rosa attends? Why?

2. Do you think there are many jobs in the medical field? Why or why not?

Now find two ads for schools in the telephone directory for your community. How are the ads the same as or different from the ones above?

Read and Write: Spotlight on Rosa

Read the questions. Read Rosa's letter very
quickly to find the answers. Circle the answers.

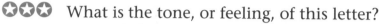

⭐ What does Rosa write about?
a. work
b. Miguel
c. the United States

⭐⭐ How does she feel about the present?
a. She thinks it's pretty.
b. She thinks it's expensive.
c. She doesn't like it.

⭐⭐⭐ What is the tone, or feeling, of this letter?
a. worried   b. cheerful   c. sad

Read the letter again carefully.

Dear Flora,

Miguel just came to visit. His visit made me homesick. I really miss you.

Miguel brought me a necklace. It was his mother's. It was his grandmother's before that. It is beautiful.

Miguel asked me to marry him! But he wants me to come back to Puebla.

He won't come here because he doesn't want to start his career all over again.

I want to stay here and open my own restaurant someday.

I was happy to see him, but now I am depressed. His work is more important to him than my work. We are not going to get married.

Love, Rosa

Find the words in the reading. What do they mean? Circle the answers.

⭐ Rosa is **homesick.**
a. She is not well.
b. Her home is hurt.
c. She misses people at home.

⭐⭐ Miguel doesn't want to start his **career** all over again.
a. work   b. schooling   c. language study

⭐⭐⭐ Rosa is **depressed.**
a. She is happy.   b. She is not happy.   c. She is not getting married.

Now you write a letter. Give the following information.

⭐ Someone gave you a present. Thank the person. Tell why you like the gift.

⭐⭐ Someone wants you to do something. You don't want to do it. Tell why you don't want to do it.

⭐⭐⭐ Talk about feelings in the letter. First you feel happy. Then something happens. You feel sad. Tell how your feelings have changed and why.

Read your letter to someone. Then ask: Did you understand? Do you have questions?

What Do You Think?

✪ Why do you think Rosa and Miguel are "Worlds Apart?" Check your answer. You may check more than one.

☐ She lives in the United States and he lives in Mexico.

☐ She works in a restaurant and he is an architect.

☐ She wants to work, but he wants her to marry him.

☐ Rosa has changed.

☐ He doesn't want to move to the United States and she doesn't want to move back to Puebla.

✪✪ Look at the sentences below. Check (✓) I agree, I disagree, or I don't know.

	I agree.	I disagree.	I don't know.
1. *If you want to succeed in Puebla, you have to think like the people who live there.*	☐	☐	☐
2. *If I moved here, I would have to start my career all over again.*	☐	☐	☐
3. *What happened last night was about living in two very different worlds.*	☐	☐	☐

✪✪✪ Answer the questions. Then read your answers to someone.

1. To succeed in a place, do you have to think like the people who live there? Tell why or why not.

_____

2. Do you think Miguel would have to start his career all over again if he moved here? Tell why or why not.

_____

3. Do you think Rosa and Miguel live in two different worlds? Tell why or why not.

_____

Culture Clip: Comparing U.S. Immigration Over Time

✪ Match.

1. At first, the U.S. was open to everyone.

a.

2. Today, immigration is more controlled.

b.

3. Immigrants of yesterday and today come for a better future.

c.

✪✪ Complete the sentences. Write one word in each blank. Use these words.

century	immigration	reasons	controlled
immigrants	survive	freedom	opportunity

The United States is a nation of immigrants. Since the early 1700s a steady stream

of people have come to this country. Throughout the 18th and most of the 19th

____century____ anyone who could _____ the travel could come. Today
    (1)   (2)

_____ is more carefully _____. But the reasons people come today are
   (3)   (4)

the same _____ the first _____ came. They are seeking _____
              (5)   (6)   (7)

and _____.
       (8)

✪✪✪ Rosa chose to stay in the United States rather than go back to her family's home in Puebla, Mexico. Miguel chose to return to Mexico rather than immigrate to the United States. How are their reasons the same or different from the people in the *Culture Clip?* Write your ideas. Then tell your ideas to someone.

_____

_____

_____

_____

Check Your English

✪ Write the correct word under each picture.

flowers
suitcase
pillow
necklace
roommate
plan

1. _____ 2. __flowers__ 3. _____ 4. _____ 5. _____ 6. _____

✪✪ Make a sentence or question from each group of words.

1. want   what   eat   do   to   you

   _What do you want to eat?_____

2. I   chicken   the   want

   _____

3. home   I   come   you   to   want

   _____

4. back   Rosa   want   go   doesn't   to   home

   _____

✪✪✪ Finish the story. Use the words in the box. Write one word in each blank.

Rosa's boyfriend Miguel comes to ___visit___ her. He asks her to marry
                                      (1)

him. She doesn't know if she is ready to _____. There are still many
                                            (2)

things she _____ to do. She is learning a lot in her business class and
              (3)

at the _____. In fact, she wants to open her own restaurant some day.
          (4)

Miguel say he will help Rosa _____ a restaurant in Puebla. She works
                                 (5)

on _____ for the restaurant. She wants an international _____.
      (6)   (7)

Miguel doesn't think an _____ restaurant would be successful in
                            (8)

Puebla. She wants the _____ in the same room with the customers.
                          (9)

Miguel says _____ don't want to watch the food being cooked.
                (10)

Rosa says she and Miguel are living in two very _____ worlds. She
                                                    (11)

decides she doesn't want to _____ to Puebla. Miguel thinks Rosa has
                               (12)

changed.

close
different
go back
international
kitchen
marry
menu
open
people
plans
restaurant
school
similar
visit
wants

4 Who's the Boss?

In this unit you will:

- make apologies
- read a newspaper ad
- write a restaurant review
- describe strategies for making a job change

Ways to Learn

Jamal *makes plans* to attend a party. He leaves work early and picks up a babysitter. *To plan* means to *prepare* or *get ready*.

Make a Plan

Check (✓) what you do to *plan* your English study.

- ☐ I study in the same place every day.
- ☐ I find a quiet place to work.
- ☐ I make a weekly study schedule.
- ☐ I study with a partner or group.
- ☐ I set a time to study every day.
- ☐ other: _____

On Your Own

How did you *plan* your study last week? _____

_____

Where did you study? _____

_____

When did you study? _____

_____

Before You Watch

Look at the pictures. What do you see?

1.

2.

3.

4.

5.

6.

✪ What do you see in each picture? Write the number of the picture next to the word.

_6_ newspaper   ____ glasses

____ wires   ____ coffee pot

____ menu   ____ notebook

✪✪ What is happening? Write the number of the picture next to the sentence.

_5_ The man at the table writes as he talks to Jamal.

____ Two men look at menus.

____ Jess looks angry as he talks to Katherine.

____ Jess reads a newspaper article.

____ Jamal is fixing something.

____ Jamal and Jihan go to a party.

✪✪✪ Write one question you have about each picture. Then read your questions to someone.

1. _Why does Jess look angry?_ _____

2. _____

3. _____

4. _____

5. _____

6. _____

Focus For Watching   Read the questions. Then watch.

✪ 1. Who visits Jamal at the café?
     2. Who goes to a party with Jamal?
     3. Who tells a lie to his friends?

✪✪ 1. Who writes for the newspaper?
     2. Who pretends to be the handyman?

✪✪✪ 1. Who waits for a phone call from the newspaper?
     2. Who asks Mr. Brashov questions about Crossroads Café?

After You Watch

What do you remember? Match each question with the correct picture. You can use a picture more than once.

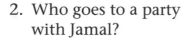 1. Who visits Jamal at the café?

a. Reporter

2. Who goes to a party with Jamal?

b. Jamal

3. Who tells a lie to his friends?

c. Mr. Brashov

✪✪ 1. Who writes for the newspaper?

2. Who pretends to be the handyman?

d. Jihan

✪✪✪ 1. Who waits for a phone call from the newspaper?

2. Who asks Mr. Brashov questions about Crossroads Café?

e. Abdullah   Mohammed

✪ Read the sentence. Circle Yes or No.

1. Jamal goes to a rock concert.   YES   (NO)
2. A reporter comes to Crossroads Café.   YES   NO
3. Jamal tells his friends that he is the boss at Crossroads Café.   YES   NO
4. There is a story about the café in the newspaper.   YES   NO

✪✪ Put the sentences in order. Number 1 to 4.

_____   Abdullah and Mohammed go to see Jamal at Crossroads Café.

__1__   Jamal sees his friends, Abdullah and Mohammed, at a party.

_____   Jamal can't tell his friends that he is only a handyman.

_____   At the café, Jamal pretends that he is the boss.

✪✪✪ Write the story. Use the four sentences above. Add these three sentences.
Then close the book and tell the story to someone.

- Jamal tells them he is in the restaurant business.
- After a while, Jamal finally tells his friends that he is the handyman and
  not the boss.
- When they meet him, they ask him about his job.

_____Jamal sees his friends, Abdullah and Mohammed at a party. When they meet him, they ask_____

him about his job._____

_____

_____

_____

_____

_____

_____

_____

_____

_____

Your New Language: Making Apologies

I'm sorry that I lied.

To apologize when you do something wrong, you can say:
- **I'm sorry that** I **came** late.
- **I'm sorry that** I **got** angry with you.

You can also say:
- **I'm sorry for** ly**ing**.
- **I'm sorry for** com**ing** late.

★ Complete the conversations. Use these words.

talked   couldn't   called   forgot

1. I'm sorry that I _forgot_ to order coffee.

That's O.K. Mr. Brashov, we have enough for today.

2. I'm sorry that I _____ find the problem with the alarm.

Do you think you can fix it today?

3. Victor, I'm sorry that I _____ you so late last night. I needed to talk.

Don't worry, my friend. Any time you need me, I am here to help.

4. Mr. Al-Jibali, I'm sorry that I _____ to you like that.

That's all right, Victor. I understand.

✪✪ Match.

1. I'm sorry for leaving the window open.
2. I'm sorry for not calling the supplier last week.
3. I'm sorry that I put a lot of salt in the soup.
4. I'm sorry for getting angry with you about my hearing problem.

a. That's O.K. The customer says it's delicious.
b. I just hope that nobody came into the café last night.
c. The important thing is that your ears are fine.
d. That's O.K. I will talk to him today about the order.

✪✪✪ Complete the conversation. Use these words. Write one in each blank. You may use a word more than once.

felt   that   lied   telling
sorry   lying

JIHAN: Why didn't you say something to your friends?

JAMAL: I'm sorry ___that___ I _____. But I was embarrassed. I didn't
          (1)   (2)
        want them to know that I was only a handyman.

JIHAN: Why? Jamal, you always work very hard. You should be proud of the work
        you do.

JAMAL: I'm _____ that I _____ ashamed of my job. But I am an
            (3)   (4)
        engineer, not a handyman!

JIHAN: Don't worry. You'll be an engineer again soon.

JAMAL: I'm sorry for not _____ the truth to my friends. I hope they
                              (5)
        understand.

JIHAN: Of course, they understand. Your friends like you for who you are.

JAMAL: I hope so. But I feel I should say I'm _____ for _____
                                                  (6)   (7)
        about my job.

✪ Put the conversation in order. Number 1 to 4.

____	JAMAL:	I told you I was the owner. But I am only the handyman.
____	ABDULLAH:	How? What did you say?
____	ABDULLAH:	Don't worry, Jamal. We like you for who you are.
__1__	JAMAL:	I'm sorry that I lied.

✪✪ Put the conversation in order. Number 1 to 5.

____	JAMAL:	But Mr. Brashov, I have another question to ask you.
____	JAMAL:	Yes, I guess so. We can talk later.
____	JAMAL:	Mr. Brashov, can I talk with you for a moment?
____	MR. BRASHOV:	I'm sorry, Jamal. I can't talk to you right now.
____	MR. BRASHOV:	Can it wait until later? First I need to finish the supply list.

✪✪✪ Put the conversation in order. Number 1 to 7.

____	MR. BRASHOV:	I don't want to talk here. Let's go to the back room. Then we can have some privacy.
____	JESS:	No, I don't think so. My hearing is just fine.
____	MR. BRASHOV:	Can I talk to you for a minute, my friend?
____	MR. BRASHOV:	Jess, I think you may have a hearing problem.
____	JESS:	What do you want to talk about?
____	MR. BRASHOV:	I'm sorry, Jess, I don't think it is. Maybe you should have it checked.
____	JESS:	O.K. Now we are alone. What do you want to say?

In Your Community: Newspaper Ads

Mr. Brashov puts an ad in the newspaper. Answer the questions about the ad. Then tell your answers to someone.

Crossroads Café

2950 West 53rd St.
Middletown, IL 12345

(217) 555-2345

Enjoy good food at great prices!

*Soups*Salads*Sandwiches
*Homemade Breads
* Delicious Desserts

Eat in and take out menus available
Free delivery for orders over $10.00
Daily senior citizen discounts– 1:00-3:00 p.m.

Sunday 7:00 a.m.-1:00 p.m.
Monday (Closed)Tuesday - Saturday 7:00 a.m.-3:00 p.m.
Sunday breakfast special 10 a.m - 1 p.m. - $6.95 per person
Major credit cards accepted

★ 1. Where is the restaurant? _____

2. What is the price of the Sunday breakfast special? _____

3. What day is the restaurant closed? _____

4. When does the restaurant open each day? _____

★★ 1. Is the restaurant open on Sunday night?   Yes   No   Sometimes

2. Can you use a credit card to pay for your meal?   Yes   No   Sometimes

3. Can you order your breakfast to take-out?   Yes   No   Sometimes

★★★ 1. You are a senior citizen and eat your lunch at 1:30 P.M. Can you get a discount for your meal?   Yes   No   Sometimes

2. You call Crossroads Café and order your lunch by phone. Your bill for lunch is $8.45. Will you have to pay to have your food brought to your house?   Yes   No   Sometimes

Tell why or why not. _____

_____

Find two restaurant ads. How are the ads that you have different from the ad for Crossroads Café? Are your restaurants more expensive? Do the ads show more prices? What are the specials? Would you like to eat at these places? Why or why not? Tell your answers to someone.

Read and Write: Spotlight on Crossroads Café

Read the questions. Read the reporter's review very quickly to find the answers. Circle the answers.

⭐ What does the reporter write about?
   a. an interview with Mr. Brashov
   b. his meal at the café
   c. his time in the neighborhood

⭐⭐ How does the reporter feel about Crossroads Café?
   a. satisfied
   b. angry
   c. unhappy

⭐⭐⭐ What is the tone or feeling of this letter?
   a. sad   b. worried   c. happy

Read the review again carefully.

Dear Readers:
I went to Crossroads Café on Wednesday for lunch. My friend and I were quickly seated at a small table. The waitress asked us about drinks and told us about the lunch specials.

While we waited, the busboy brought bread, hot from the oven. Delicious! The wait was short. I ordered the spicy chicken and rice and my friend, who is a vegetarian, ordered pasta and vegetables. The service was excellent. Our meals came in no time at all. The food was hot and delicious. There was too much food to finish. We asked for "doggy bags" to take leftovers home. Then we had a slice of chocolate cake for dessert. It was O.K., but a little dry, in my opinion.

Our bill was $23.54, a good price. I highly recommend Crossroads Café for anyone. They have good food, good service, friendly staff, and good prices.

Find the words in the reading. What do they mean? Circle the answer.

⭐ A **dessert** is:
   a. something you eat at the beginning of a meal
   b. the last thing you eat in a meal like cake, ice cream, or fruit
   c. something that you eat with a salad

⭐⭐ A **"doggy bag"** is:
   a. a bag used to take extra food home from a restaurant
   b. a bag that dog food comes in
   c. a bag that stores use to put meat in

⭐⭐⭐ A **vegetarian** is:
   a. a person who eats only plant foods or vegetables
   b. a person who does not like vegetables
   c. a person who does not eat dinner

Now you write a review of a restaurant or a food place. In your review, answer the following questions.

⭐ 1. What is the name of the restaurant?
2. Where is it?
3. What kinds of food can you get there?

⭐⭐ 1. What is your favorite food at this place? Why?
2. How much does it cost for a meal?
3. How often do you go to the restaurant?

⭐⭐⭐ 1. What are two things that a vegetarian could eat in this restaurant?
2. How is the service?
3. What recommendations would you make about this place?
Tell why.

Read your restaurant review to someone. Then ask: Did you understand? Do you have questions?

What Do You Think?

✪ Why didn't Jamal tell his friends he was the handyman?
- ☐ He was embarrassed.
- ☐ He thought his friends would not like him.
- ☐ He doesn't like working at Crossroads Café.
- ☐ He feels bad because he doesn't have an engineering job.
- ☐ He feels bad about getting laid off.

✪✪ Look at the sentences below. Check (✓) I agree, I disagree, or I don't know.

	I agree.	I disagree.	I don't know.
1. Jamal, you should never be ashamed of the work you do.	☐	☐	☐
2. I like people for who they are, not how successful they are.	☐	☐	☐
3. You should have told your friends the truth.	☐	☐	☐

✪✪✪ Answer the questions. Then read your answers to someone.

1. Do you think Jamal should be ashamed of the work he does? Tell why or why not.

_____

2. Do you like people for who they are or for how successful they are? Tell why.

_____

3. Do you think Jamal should have told his friends the truth? Tell why or why not.

_____

Culture Clip: Career Changes

✪ Match.

1. Sometimes people can't find jobs in their professions.

2. Sometimes big companies lay off people from their jobs.

3. Programs help people who have lost their jobs.

4. After retraining, some people are happy with their new jobs.

a.

b.

c.

d.

✪✪ Complete the paragraph about job changes. Use these words.

beginning	countries	difficult	experiences	home
industries	jobs	laid off	occupations	programs
reasons	retraining	step	support	

Some people find themselves without ___jobs___ for very different _____. When people
                                        (1)   (2)

move to new _____, they often cannot find the same jobs they held in their _____
                (3)   (4)

country. Other people get _____ from big _____. They often turn to _____
                            (5)   (6)   (7)

programs for help. Retraining _____ provide both training and _____ for men and
                                (8)   (9)

women at a _____ time in their lives. The programs help people look at _____
             (10)   (11)

different from their former work. For some people in new jobs, each day offers new _____.
                                                                                     (12)

For others, it is only the _____.
                            (13)

✪✪✪ Think.

When people change jobs for whatever reasons, they often have many different feelings.
List some feelings people may have when they lose their jobs. Have you ever had any
of these feelings? What are some of the things that you did to get another job?

Check Your English

✪ Write the correct word under each picture.

wires

coffee pot

glass

newspaper

menu

notebook

1. _coffee pot_

2. _____

3. _____

4. _____

5. _____

6. _____

✪✪ Make a sentence from each group of words.

1. sorry   truth   the   tell   I'm   I   didn't   that

I'm sorry that I didn't tell the truth.

2. for   we're   coming   your   late   sorry   we   party   to

_____

3. alarm   I'm   that   fix   couldn't   sorry   I   the

_____

4. making   sorry   kitchen   I'm   the   a   for   mess   in

_____

✪✪✪ Finish the story. Use the words in the box. Write one word in each blank.

Jamal meets his friends, Abdullah and Mohammed, at a party. When they
meet him, they ask him about his ___job___ . When Jamal knew them, he
(1)
was an _____ . He can't tell his friends that now he is only a _____ .
(2)   (3)
So he tells them he is in the _____ business. Abdullah and Mohammed
(4)
go to see Jamal at Crossroads Café. At the café, Jamal pretends that he is the
_____ . Everyone at the café _____ Jamal when he is the boss.
(5)   (6)
Mr. Brashov _____ to be the handyman. Jamal _____ bad for
(7)   (8)
what he has done. After awhile, he finally_____ his _____ that
(9)   (10)
he is not the boss. Mohammed and Abdullah tell Jamal they don't care how
_____ he is. They like him for who he is.
(11)

boss
embarrassed
engineer
feels
finally
friends
handyman
hearing
helps
job
party
pretends
problem
restaurant
successful
tells

5 Lost and Found

In this unit you will:

- tell someone to do something
- read about home security
- write a letter describing a burglary
- describe ways to prevent neighborhood crime

Ways to Learn

Jess and Carol *use resources* to keep their home safe. They *ask people* for help and *read about* ways to prevent a burglary. Books are *resources*. People are *resources*.

Use Resources

Circle the *resources* you use to learn English.

1. Find the meaning of a word
   a. dictionary
   b. friend
2. Spell a word
   a. dictionary
   b. family member
3. Practice English pronunciation
   a. teacher
   b. dictionary
4. Practice English grammar
   a. textbook
   b. friend

On Your Own

What *resources* did you use last week to learn English? List the *resources* and tell how helpful they were.

Resource	Circle One	
_____	helpful	not helpful
_____	helpful	not helpful
_____	helpful	not helpful

Before You Watch

Look at the pictures. What do you see?

1.

2.

3.

4.

5.

6.

✪ What do you see in each picture? Write the number of the picture next to the word.

  _6_   neighbors   _____ police officer

_____ security devices   _____ burglary

_____ alarm system   _____ salesperson

✪✪ What is happening? Write the number of the picture next to the sentence.

_____ A man is showing a security device to Jess and Carol.

_____ The neighbors come to Carol's house.

_____ There are many security devices on the table.

 _1_ There has been a burglary at Carol and Jess's home.

_____ Jamal is helping Jess.

_____ The police officer is talking to Carol and Jess.

✪✪✪ Write one question you have about each picture. Then read your questions to someone.

1. What was taken from their home? _____

2. _____

3. _____

4. _____

5. _____

6. _____

Focus For Watching   Read the questions. Then watch.

✪ 1. Who has a burglary?
    2. Who brings the security devices to Jess and Carol's home?

✪✪ 1. Who helps install a home security device?
     2. Who invites the neighbors to a meeting?

✪✪✪ 1. Who is worried about Carol being out late?

After You Watch

What do you remember? Match each question with the correct picture. You can use a picture more than once.

✪ 1. Who has a burglary?

a. Jamal

2. Who brings the security devices to Jess and Carol's home?

b. Jess

✪✪ 1. Who helps install a home security device?

c. Jess and Carol

2. Who invites the neighbors to a meeting?

d. salesperson

✪✪✪ 1. Who is worried about Carol being out late?

e. Carol

✪ Read the sentences. Circle Yes or No.
1. The burglars take the VCR and toaster oven.   (YES)   NO
2. Carol and Jess buy security devices from the salesperson.   YES   NO
3. The alarm system works very well.   YES   NO
4. The police officer talks with Carol and Jess and writes a report.   YES   NO

✪✪ Put the sentences in order. Number 1 to 5.

_____   Jess doesn't buy any devices because they are too expensive.

_____   A police officer comes and takes a crime report.

_____   Carol and the neighbors meet to discuss crime prevention in their neighborhood.

__1__   There is a burglary at Jess and Carol's house.

_____   Jess has a salesperson come to show him security devices.

✪✪✪ Write the story. Use the five sentences above. Add these three sentences. Then close the book and tell the story to someone.
- The alarm system does not work.
- He buys a do-it-yourself alarm kit and asks Jamal to help him.
- He asks for a description of the items that were stolen.

There is a burglary at Jess and Carol's house. _____

_____

_____

_____

_____

_____

_____

_____

_____

_____

_____

_____

Your New Language: Telling Someone to Do Something

To tell someone to do something you can say:

• **Give** me the ball.

To say it more politely, you can add **please**:

• **Please give** me the ball.

⭐ Complete the conversations. Use these words and phrases.

out of here   ears   the ball   the blue wire

1.

Come on, throw me __the ball__.

2.

Get _____!

3.

Place the green wire beneath _____.

4.

Cover your _____.

62 ===== Crossroads Café   Worktext A

✪✪ Match.
1. Wait up, guys.
2. Put the keys in
   your purse.
3. Punch in the code for
   the burglary alarm system.
4. Put the hammer down.
   Is it yours?
5. Be patient. He's young.

a. I don't carry one.
b. No, it isn't.

c. You're right. He'll grow
   out of it.
d. O.K., but hurry.

e. What's the number?

✪✪✪ Complete the conversation. Use these words and phrases. Write one in each
blank. You may use a word or phrase more than once.

set	don't make	come	clean
do	do not leave	keep	talk
don't be			

KATHERINE: O.K. David. Here are the new rules. _____Come_____ home right after
                                                      (1)

school. _____ your homework, first. Then, _____ your
                (2)   (3)

room and _____ the table for dinner. _____ the house
                (4)   (5)

and _____ to no one on the phone until I get home.
            (6)

DAVID: Come on, mom. _____ so hard on me.
                              (7)

KATHERINE: _____ this up and you'll find yourself in military school.
                  (8)

            _____ me do that.
                  (9)

DAVID: O.K. O.K.

✪ Put the conversation in order. Number 1 to 3

_____ JOSH: Oh, O.K. Give me the ball, please.

__1__ JOSH: Come on, mister. Give me the ball!

_____ MR. BRASHOV: I will not give you the ball until you say "please."

✪✪ Put the conversation in order. Number 1 to 4.

_____ JAMAL: You can come in in a few minutes. Please, cover your ears. It will be very loud.

_____ JAMAL: Mrs. Washington, go outside and close the door. I'll set the alarm.

_____ CAROL: O.K. Let me know when I can come in.

_____ CAROL: I will. Knock when you're ready.

✪✪✪ Put the conversation in order. Number 1 to 6.

_____ CAROL: It's very heavy. But steel bars remind me of jail.

_____ JESS: Sure. Carol, move the plants and I'll get the lamp.

_____ SALESPERSON: I have several security devices. I'll need to use your table to lay them all out.

_____ SALESPERSON: Thanks. This is perfect. Pick up the steel bar, Mrs. Washington. What do you think?

_____ SALESPERSON: If you don't like the bars, then install one of these alarm systems. Take a look at this one. It includes a closed-circuit camera.

_____ JESS: Thanks for coming, Mr. Kincaid. What can you show us?

In Your Community

Read the following Crime Prevention pamphlet the police officer gave Carol and Jess. Answer Yes or No for each question and circle the information in the pamphlet that helped you choose the answer.

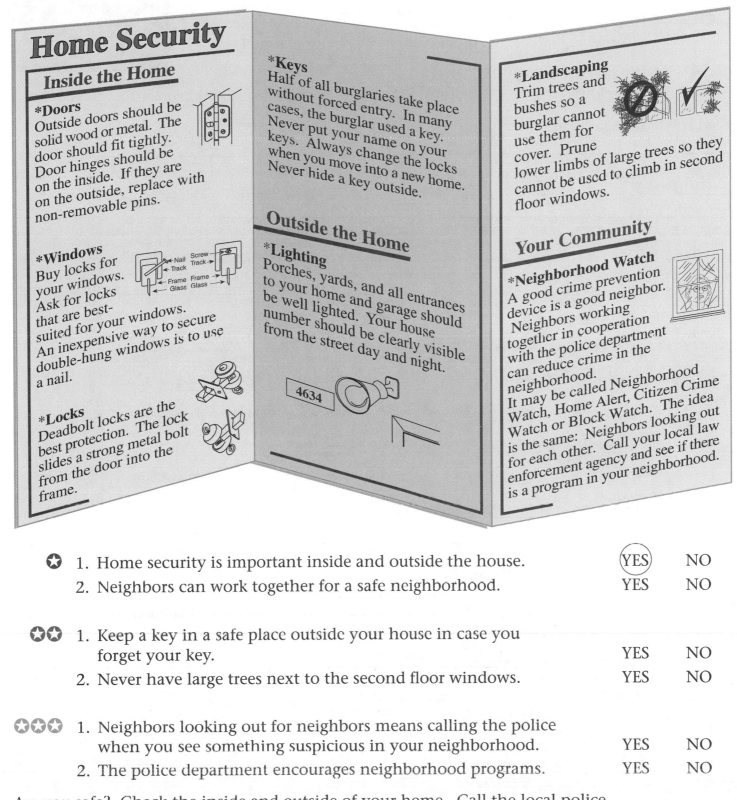

Home Security

Inside the Home

*Doors
Outside doors should be solid wood or metal. The door should fit tightly. Door hinges should be on the inside. If they are on the outside, replace with non-removable pins.

*Windows
Buy locks for your windows. Ask for locks that are best-suited for your windows. An inexpensive way to secure double-hung windows is to use a nail.

*Locks
Deadbolt locks are the best protection. The lock slides a strong metal bolt from the door into the frame.

*Keys
Half of all burglaries take place without forced entry. In many cases, the burglar used a key. Never put your name on your keys. Always change the locks when you move into a new home. Never hide a key outside.

Outside the Home

*Lighting
Porches, yards, and all entrances to your home and garage should be well lighted. Your house number should be clearly visible from the street day and night.

*Landscaping
Trim trees and bushes so a burglar cannot use them for cover. Prune lower limbs of large trees so they cannot be used to climb in second floor windows.

Your Community

*Neighborhood Watch
A good crime prevention device is a good neighbor. Neighbors working together in cooperation with the police department can reduce crime in the neighborhood. It may be called Neighborhood Watch, Home Alert, Citizen Crime Watch or Block Watch. The idea is the same: Neighbors looking out for each other. Call your local law enforcement agency and see if there is a program in your neighborhood.

⭐ 1. Home security is important inside and outside the house. (YES) NO

2. Neighbors can work together for a safe neighborhood. YES NO

⭐⭐ 1. Keep a key in a safe place outside your house in case you forget your key. YES NO

2. Never have large trees next to the second floor windows. YES NO

⭐⭐⭐ 1. Neighbors looking out for neighbors means calling the police when you see something suspicious in your neighborhood. YES NO

2. The police department encourages neighborhood programs. YES NO

Are you safe? Check the inside and outside of your home. Call the local police department to see if there is a crime prevention program in your neighborhood.

Read and Write: Spotlight on Jess

Read the questions. Read Jess's letter very quickly to find the answers. Circle the answers.

✪ What does Jess write about?
   a. his wife's jewelry   b. the burglary   c. his anniversary

✪✪ How does he feel?
   a. upset   b. sad   c. unalarmed

✪✪✪ What is the tone of the letter?
   a. serious   b. cautious   c. both serious and cautious

Read the letter again carefully.

> Dear Son,
>
>   I'm writing you a note to say hello and to tell you some unfortunate news. Don't worry, everything is fine now. But, a few days ago we had a burglary at the house. Someone broke in and took our VCR, radio, and some jewelry. Also, can you believe they took the toaster oven? The burglar got in through the sliding glass door. We're glad we were not home. Your mother was so sad about losing her diamond earrings—the ones I gave her for our 10th anniversary. We were so upset we called a security device salesperson. He came and we looked at a lot of alarms. But, they were too expensive. Your mom has gathered a few neighbors together. We plan to form a neighborhood watch committee. I think this will help.
>
>   I want you to be very careful. Lock your doors and windows and always keep the lights on when you are not home. I know I worry too much.
>
> Love, Dad
>
> P.S. I know what I'll be getting your mother for our next anniversary!!!

Find the words or phrases in the note that are similar to the words or phrases below.
Write your answers in the blanks.

✪ 1. diamond earrings = _____jewelry_____

   2. sad and angry = _____

✪✪ 1. bad = _____

   2. letter = _____

✪✪✪ 1. brought together = _____

   2. entered a house illegally = _____

Now you write a note to someone about a burglary. In your note answer the following questions.

✪ 1. Who had a burglary?
2. Where was the burglary?
3. What did the burglar take?

✪✪ 1. When did it happen?
2. How did it happen?
3. What did the person who was robbed do?

✪✪✪ 1. What would you do if it happened to you?

Dear   ,

What Do You Think?

✪ What do you think is the best way for Carol and Jess to keep their home safe? Number 1 and 2.

_____ neighborhood meeting

_____ security devices

✪✪ Look at the sentences below. Check (✓) I agree, I disagree, or I don't know.

	I agree.	I disagree.	I don't know.
1.	☐	☐	☐
2.	☐	☐	☐

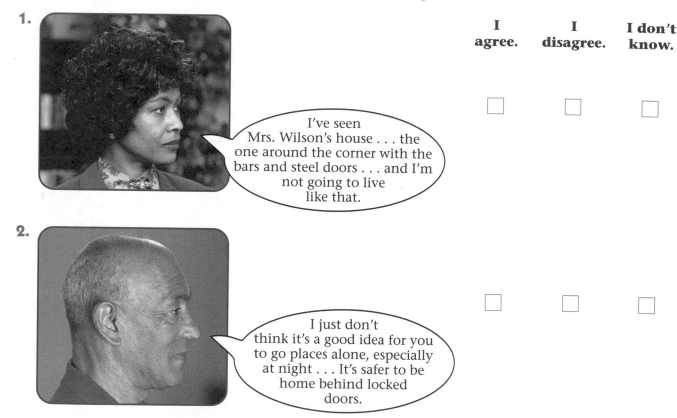

1. I've seen Mrs. Wilson's house . . . the one around the corner with the bars and steel doors . . . and I'm not going to live like that.

2. I just don't think it's a good idea for you to go places alone, especially at night . . . It's safer to be home behind locked doors.

✪✪✪ Answer the questions. Then read your answers to someone.

1. Do you think people should secure their homes with bars and steel doors? Tell why or why not.

_____

2. Do you think women should go out alone at night? Tell why or why not.

_____

Culture Clip: Neighbors Working to Prevent Crime

⭐ Match.

1. Neighbors join together to protect their neighborhood.

a.

2. They clean up graffiti.

b.

3. They report crimes to police.

c.

4. Police officers advise, "Don't fight a robber."

d.

⭐⭐ Complete the sentences. Write one word in each blank. Use these words.

| neighbors | meetings | report | community |
| prevent | graffiti | police | protect |

Across the United States _neighbors_ are working together to _____ crime.
　　　　　　　　　　　　　　　(1)　　　　　　　　　　　　　　　　　　　　(2)
They form Neighborhood Watch groups. These groups _____ crimes and clean
　　　　　　　　　　　　　　　　　　　　　　　　　　　　　　(3)
up _____. They have _____ and invite the police. The _____ help
　　　(4)　　　　　　　　　　(5)　　　　　　　　　　　　　　　　(6)
members _____ themselves from crime. Neighborhood Watch works very well.
　　　　　　(7)
When groups are formed in a _____, crime drops significantly.
　　　　　　　　　　　　　　　(8)

⭐⭐⭐ Carol invites her neighbors to her house to form a Neighborhood Watch group. Do you think these groups make a difference in the community? Why or why not? Write your ideas. Then tell your ideas to someone.

_____

_____

Check Your English

✪ Write the correct word under each picture.

alarm system
security devices
salesperson
police officer
burglary
neighbors

1.  2.  3.

___burglary___ _____ _____

4.  5. _____ 6. _____

_____

✪✪ Make a sentence from each group of words.

1. button   push   and   your   cover   the   ears

   Push the button and cover your ears.
   _____

2. and   be   sit   quiet   down   please

   _____

3. the   doors   the   windows   lock   and

   _____

4. night   please   out   late   don't   stay   at

   _____

✪✪✪ Finish the story. Use the words in the box. Write one word in each blank.

Jess and Carol are very upset. There is a __burglary__ at their home. The
                                              (1)
_____ take a VCR and toaster oven. A police officer comes to write a
   (2)
_____. Jess is very upset about the burglary. He calls a _____ to
   (3)   (4)
come and show him a variety of _____. Carol does not want to live in
                                   (5)
a jail and is not interested in the devices. Jess does not like the _____.
                                                                        (6)
The deluxe security system is too _____. Jess buys a do-it-yourself
                                     (7)
alarm kit and asks Jamal to help him _____ it. The system doesn't
                                         (8)
work. Carol has a better solution. She has a _____ with her neighbors
                                                (9)
to discuss crime _____. It's much less expensive.
                    (10)

airplane
burglars
burglary
crime
report
expensive
install
meeting
neighbors
prevention
price
salesperson
security
devices

Time Is Money

In this unit you will:

- make suggestions
- read schedules
- write a letter
- recognize U.S. attitude about time

Ways to Learn

Mr. Brashov wants *to organize* his paperwork. Mr. Bradford helps him *organize* by sorting papers.

Organize Your Study

Check (✓) ways you *organize* your English study.

- ☐ I keep my English books in one place.
- ☐ I keep a notebook for new words.
- ☐ I make a list of what I need to learn.
- ☐ I keep a file of completed work.
- ☐ other: _____

On Your Own

Last week how did you *organize* your study?

_____

Where did you study? _____

What time did you study each day? _____

Did you make a list?	YES	NO
Did you keep a notebook?	YES	NO
Did you keep your books in one place?	YES	NO

Before You Watch

Look at the pictures. What do you see?

1.

2.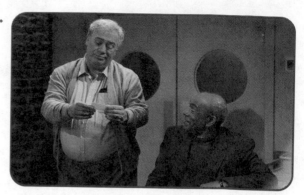

3.

4.

5.

6.

✪ What do you see in each picture? Write the number of the picture next to the word.

_2_ business card   ____ telephone

____ chart   ____ trophy

____ paperwork   ____ watch

✪✪ What is happening? Write the number of the picture next to the sentence.

_6_ The man leaves with a trophy.

____ A man times Katherine with a watch.

____ Mr. Brashov has a lot of paperwork.

____ The man talks about a chart.

____ Jess gives Mr. Brashov a business card.

____ The man writes and Mr. Brashov talks on the telephone.

✪✪✪ Write one question you have about each picture. Then read your questions to someone.

1. What is wrong with Mr. Brashov? _____

2. _____

3. _____

4. _____

5. _____

6. _____

Focus For Watching   Read the questions. Then watch.

✪ 1. Who has a problem?
     2. Who comes to help?

✪✪ 1. Who suggests someone to help?
     2. Who wins the contest?

✪✪✪ 1. Who wants to win the contest?
     2. Who saves money by comparing prices?

After You Watch

What do you remember? Match each question with the correct picture. You can use a picture more than once.

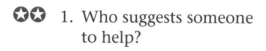 1. Who has a problem?

a. Rosa

2. Who comes to help?

b. Jamal

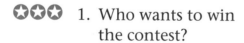 1. Who suggests someone to help?

c. Mr. Brashov

2. Who wins the contest?

d. Katherine

⭐⭐⭐ 1. Who wants to win the contest?

e. Jess

2. Who saves money by comparing prices?

f. Mr. Bradford

✪ Read the sentences. Circle Yes or No.
1. Mr. Brashov likes paperwork.   YES   (NO)
2. Jamal suggests someone to help Mr. Brashov.   YES   NO
3. Mr. Bradford wants everyone to work quickly.   YES   NO
4. Katherine wins the contest.   YES   NO

✪✪ Put the sentences in order. Number 1 to 4.

_____   Emery Bradford helps Mr. Brashov organize his paperwork.

__1__   Mr. Brashov has too much paperwork.

_____   Mr. Brashov does not like the changes or the contest.

_____   Mr. Bradford has a contest for the most efficient employee.

✪✪✪ Write the story. Use the four sentences above. Add these three sentences.
Then close the book and tell the story to someone.

• He has too many bills and too many receipts.

• He wants to make people work faster.

• When Mr. Bradford leaves, Mr. Brashov and his employees are happy.

Mr. Brashov has too much paperwork. He has too many bills and too many receipts.

_____

_____

_____

_____

_____

_____

_____

_____

_____

_____

_____

Your New Language: Making Suggestions

Mr. Brashov, you look hungry. Why don't you have lunch?

Thank you, Rosa, but I don't have time to eat.

To make suggestions, you can say:

- **Why don't you . . .** have some lunch?
- **Maybe you should . . .** have some lunch.
- **How about . . .** having some lunch?

⭐ Complete the conversations. Use these words.

go to the library   make a schedule   have another cup   take off your headphones

1.

I can't hear you.

Why don't you _take off your_ _headphones_ ?

2.

I need to study.

Why don't you _____ ?

3.

This coffee is very good.

Why don't you _____ ?

4.

There are so many bills. I can't remember when to pay them

Why don't you _____ ?

✪✪ Match.

1. I'm cold.
2. I can't watch Crossroads Café this week.
3. The air conditioner is broken.
4. I have an examination next week.
5. I need to practice speaking English with someone.

a. Why don't you videotape it?
b. How about closing the window?
c. Maybe you should study.
d. How about getting a study partner?
e. Maybe you should fix it.

✪✪✪ Complete the conversation. Use these phrases.

How about   Why don't you   Maybe you should

ROSA: ___How about___ having lunch?
                      (1)

MR. BRASHOV: Thank you, but I don't have time to eat.

JESS: With all that paperwork, you never have time. _____ get help?
                                                                (2)

MR. BRASHOV: I don't know anyone who is good at organizing paperwork.

JESS: Here's the business card of a friend. _____ give him a call.
                                                          (3)

MR. BRASHOV: Thank you, but I think it will be too expensive.

JESS: He's a friend. He'll do it as a favor to me.

MR. BRASHOV: You mean I won't have to pay? Great! Thanks for the suggestion.

JESS: Now, _____ playing a little chess?
                        (4)

✪ Put the conversation in order. Number 1 to 3.

__1__ We need a new filter.

_____ Because filters are cheaper at Bidwell's Hardware.

_____ Why don't you get one at Joe's Hardware?

✪✪ Put the conversation in order. Number 1 to 5.

_____ I still need a way to know when to pay them.

_____ Good. I need help.

_____ First, you should divide your bills into categories—rent, supplies, utilities.

_____ I'll help you organize your paperwork.

_____ How about using this calendar to make a schedule?

✪✪✪ Put the conversation in order. Number 1 to 6.

_____ But they might be sold out.

_____ One last suggestion. Why don't you leave your headphones at home?

_____ Maybe you should buy them after work instead of before work.

_____ I'm sorry I'm late. I was buying tickets for a concert.

_____ O.K. Next time I'll call.

_____ And another thing. How about calling if you're going to be late!

In Your Community: School Schedules

This is the schedule for Rosa's school Answer the questions about the schedule.
Then tell your aswers to someone.

Spring Semester Night Classes		
Accounting	MWF	5:00-6:20 P.M.
Business Machines	W	5:30-8:20 P.M.
Business Management	M	6:30-7:50 P.M.
Computer Repair	Tu	6:30-9:20 P.M.
English	M	7:00-7:50 P.M.
English as a Second Language	TuTh	6:30-9:00 P.M.

✪ 1. What day is the Business Management class? _____

2. What time does it begin? _____

3. What time does it end? _____

✪✪ 1. How long is the Business Management class? _____

2. How often does the Accounting class meet? _____

3. How many hours a week is the English as a Second Language class? _____

✪✪✪ Can you take both the English class and the Business Management class? Tell why or
why not.

_____

_____

Now get a schedule from a school in your community. How is it the same or
different from this schedule?

Read and Write: Spotlight on Jess

Jess wrote this letter to his son. Read Jess's letter quickly to find the answers. Circle the answers.

★ What is the letter about?
   a. money   b. Jess's wife   c. Emery Bradford

★★ How does Jess feel about the café now?
   a. He likes it.   b. He doesn't like it.   c. He liked it better with Emery there.

★★★ What is the tone or feeling of the letter?
   a. angry   b. sad   c. amused

Read the letter again carefully.

Dear Son,

How are things at school? We're fine here. Your mother sends her love to you.

Well, I have some local news to tell you this week. Do you remember your old friend Emery Bradford? He helps me with my taxes, you know. I gave his business card to Mr. Brashov at the café. I thought Emery could help Mr. Brashov organize his paperwork. Mr. Brashov usually has a mountain of papers on his desk. He's a nice man, but he's very disorganized.

At first, Emery was perfect—you know he's like a machine. He organized and filed that mountain of paper in minutes. But then he really did too much. He followed the employees around with his stopwatch. He timed every movement they made. He kept repeating, "Time is money." The employees didn't like the stopwatch!

Mr. Brashov finally told Emery to stop. Thank goodness. Things are normal again—relaxed and disorganized. But I'm not sorry I gave Emery's business card to Mr. Brashov. Watching this has been a lot of fun.

Love, Dad.

P.S. Here's $10 for a haircut.

Find the words in the reading. Write the correct word on each line.

★ not arranged, not in order   _____

★★ arrange, to put in order   _____

★★★ usual   _____

Now you write a letter about Emery. In your letter answer the following questions.

✪ 1. How did Mr. Brashov find Emery?
    2. How did Emery help Mr. Brashov?

✪✪ 1. What did the employees think of Emery? Why?
    2. Did Emery help Mr. Brashov change? Tell why or why not.
    3. Why did Mr. Brashov ask Emery to leave?

✪✪✪ 1. How did Emery feel when Mr. Brashov asked him to leave?
    2. What did Emery think of the employees? Why?
    3. Do you think Emery is a better boss than Mr. Brashov? Tell why or why not.

Dear   ,

Love,

Read your letter to someone. Then ask: Did you understand? Do you have questions?

What Do You Think?

✪ What is more important to you? Circle number 1 or 2.

1.

Money is more important than people.

2.

People are more important than money.

✪✪ Look at the sentences below. Check (✓) I agree, I disagree, or I don't know.

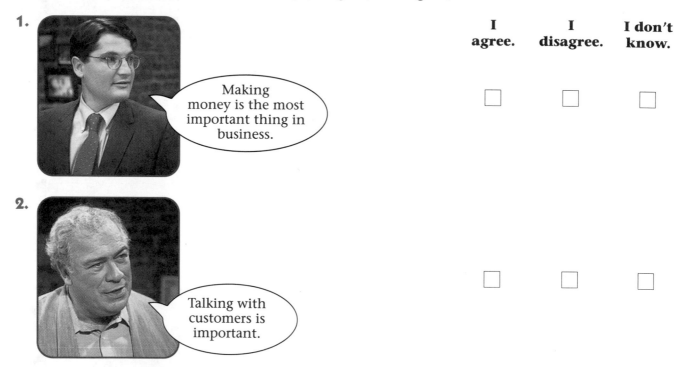

	I agree.	I disagree.	I don't know.
1. Making money is the most important thing in business.	☐	☐	☐
2. Talking with customers is important.	☐	☐	☐

✪✪✪ Answer the questions. Then read your answers to someone.

1. Do you think making money is the most important thing in business?
   Tell why or why not.

   _____

2. Do you think talking with customers is important? Tell why or why not.

   _____

Culture Clip: U.S. Attitude about Time

✪ Match.

1. Time is important in the United States.

2. Time controls the world of work.

3. Time controls transportation.

a.

b.

c.

✪✪ Complete the sentences. Write one word in each blank. Use these words.

appointment   late   needs   ticket
business   lose   sports   time

In many countries, including the United States, time controls the world of

_____business_____, the professions, transportation, and _____.
      (1)   (2)

Farmers use the sun to _____ their activities. Parents struggle
                                     (3)

against time, trying to juggle the _____ of a family and a job.
                                      (4)

To ignore time—to be _____—often causes serious problems.
                             (5)

- If you are late to work too many times, you can _____ your job.
                                                  (6)

- If you are late for a doctor's _____, you
                                   (7)
may have to make another appointment.

- If you are late returning to your car, you may get a parking _____.
                                                                         (8)

No matter how you look at it, it pays to be on time.

✪✪✪ You are Mr. Brashov. What will you do? Write your ideas. Then tell your ideas to someone.

1. Henry is late for work.
2. Rosa asks to leave work early.

Check Your English

✪ Write the correct word under each picture.

chart

trophy

watch

business card

telephone

paperwork

1.
_____

2.
_____

3.
chart

4.
_____

5.
_____

6.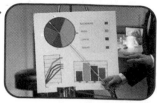
_____

✪✪ Make a sentence or question from each group of words.

1. the   should   to   you   library   maybe   go

   Maybe you should go to the library.

2. partner   studying   with   about   how   a   English

   _____

3. schedule   why   a   make   you   don't

   _____

4. help   maybe   get   should   you

   _____

✪✪✪ Finish the story. Use the words in the box. Write one word in each blank.

Mr. Brashov has a lot of ___paperwork___ to do, and he doesn't like paperwork.
(1)
Jess suggests that Emery Bradford help _____ get organized. Emery
(2)
helps Mr. Brashov organize his _____. But he also tries to _____
(3)   (4)
Crossroads Café. He wants workers who _____ time. He wants
(5)
efficient workers. _____ has a contest for the _____ efficient
(6)   (7)
worker. Mr. Bradford says Rosa _____ the winner. She says, "I
(8)
_____ accept this award. It doesn't _____ just to me. It belongs
(9)   (10)
to all of us."

be
belong
bills
can't
change
don't
he
him
his
Emery
is
more
most
organize
paperwork
save
waste

Fish Out of Water

In this unit you will:

- talk about experiences
- read a recipe
- write a postcard
- identify stages in adjusting to a new culture

Ways to Learn

Mr. Brashov *listens carefully* to his brother Nicolae. He tries to understand the *meaning* from his brother's words. Listening for meaning takes practice.

Listen for Meaning

Check (✓) ways you *listen for meaning* in conversations with family, friends, or coworkers.

- ☐ I listen to the whole conversation, not just parts.
- ☐ I listen for words or phrases I understand.
- ☐ I watch for facial expressions and gestures.
- ☐ I guess meaning when I don't understand.
- ☐ I listen for word endings (example: ed, ing, es).
- ☐ I ask for repetition.
- ☐ I ask for meanings of words or phrases.
- ☐ other:

On Your Own

I practiced *listening for meaning* last week. YES NO

Listening for meaning is difficult for me. YES NO

Listening for meaning is easier when I use the ideas from the checklist. YES NO

List ways you will *listen for meaning:*

_____

_____

_____

Before You Watch

Look at the pictures. What do you see?

1.

2.

3.

4.

5.

6.

✪ What do you see in each picture? Write the number of the picture next to the word.

_5_ poster   _2_ handkerchief

_3_ flag   _1_ banner

_4_ band   _6_ wallet

✪✪ What is happening? Write the number of the picture next to the sentence.

_5_ There is a poster on the wall.

_6_ A man gives a wallet to Mr. Brashov.

_1_ Jamal hangs a banner in the café.

_4_ Mr. Brashov is angry with some men in the café.

_2_ Mr. Brashov sneezes into a handkerchief.

_3_ There is a flag above the kitchen door.

✪✪✪ Write one question you have about each picture. Then read your questions to someone.

1. Why is Jamal hanging a banner? He wants give Welcom People

2. Why is Mr. Brashov sneezes into at

3. Why the flag is above the kitchen door

4. Why Mr. Brashov angry with some men in the

5. Poster

6. A man gives a wallet to Mr Brashov

Focus For Watching   Read the questions. Then watch.

✪ 1. Who comes to visit Mr. Brashov? Mr. Brashov cousin

2. Who plays music in the café? A band

3. Who rips up a poster of Romania?

✪✪ 1. Who gets angry about changes in the café?

2. Who does Nicolae meet in the cabaret?

✪✪✪ 1. Who finds it difficult to live in the United States?

2. Who comes to the café to return something to Mr. Brashov?

After You Watch

What do you remember? Match each question with the correct picture. You can use a picture more than once.

⭐ 1. Who comes to visit _d_
Mr. Brashov?

a. Mr. Brashov

2. Who plays music in _e_
the café?

3. Who rips up a poster
of Romania?

b. a Romanian man

⭐⭐ 1. Who gets angry about _a_
the changes in the café?

2. Who does Nicolae meet _b_
in the cabaret?

c. a man from the mall

d. Nicolae

⭐⭐⭐ 1. Who finds it difficult to _d_
live in the United States?

2. Who comes to the café to _c_
return something to Mr. Brashov?

e. Romanian band

✪ Read the sentences. Circle Yes or No.

1. Mr. Brashov's cousin comes to visit.   YES   (NO)
2. Nicolae likes living in the United States.   YES   NO
3. Mr. Brashov likes the changes in the café.   YES   NO
4. Someone stole Nicolae's wallet.   YES   NO

✪✪ Put the sentences in order. Number 1 to 4.

__2__ He wants to learn about the café so he can help Mr. Brashov.

__1__ Mr. Brashov's brother Nicolae comes to visit from Romania.

__4__ Then Nicolae leaves the United States and goes back to Romania.

__3__ While Mr. Brashov is at home, Nicolae makes some changes in the café.

✪✪✪ Write the story. Use the four sentences above. Add these three sentences.
Then close the book and tell the story to someone.

- When Mr. Brashov returns and sees what Nicolae has done, he becomes angry.
- When Mr. Brashov becomes sick, Nicolae takes charge of the café.
- The two brothers argue and Nicolae leaves the café.

Mr. Brashov's brother Nicolae comes to visit from Romania. He wants to learn about the café so he can help Mr. Brashov. When Mr. Brashov becomes sick Nicolae takes charge of the cafe While Mr. Brashov is at home, Nicolae makes some changes in the cafe. When Mr. Brashov returns and sees what Nicolae has done, he becomes angry. The two brother argue and Nicolae leaves the cafe, then Nicolae leaves the United and goes back to Romania

Your New Language: Talking about Experiences

> Can you cook rice?

> Oh yes, that's easy. I have cooked rice many times.

To talk about things that happened in the past and continue to the present, you can say:

- I **have** cook**ed** rice many times.
- Jamal **has** repair**ed** many things in the café.

⭐ Complete the conversations. Use these words.

recovered   worked   warmed   learned

1.

> Can Rosa cook stew?

> Yes, she has <u>learned</u> to cook it very well.

2.

> Is Mr. Brashov still sick?

> No, he has <u>Recovered</u> from the flu.

3.

> I am hungry.

> Good, I have <u>warmed</u> this soup for you.

4.

> What have you done to my restaurant?

> I have <u>worked</u> hard to make the café more like home.

✪✪ Match.

1. Where is Nicolae?
2. How is Nicolae doing?
3. How long have you been in the United States?
4. Do you want some soup?
5. Does Nicolae have any business experience?

a. I have been here for five years.
b. Great! He has learned a lot about the café.
c. Yes, he has managed a hotel.
d. I don't know. I haven't seen him.
e. Yes, thank you. I haven't eaten anything today.

✪✪✪ Complete the conversation. Use these words. Write one word in each blank.

eaten   done   brought   have
have learned   tried

MR. BRASHOV: What do you have there?

NICOLAE: Oh, these are for you. I have ___brought___ you some recipes from home.
(1)

MR. BRASHOV: Why have you ___Done___ that?
(2)

NICOLAE: Maybe you can make some Romanian food for the café.

MR. BRASHOV: Yes, maybe.

NICOLAE: I'm sorry, Victor. It was a stupid idea.

MR. BRASHOV: That's O.K. It's just that things are a little different here. When you ___have learned___ more about the café, it will make sense.
(3)

NICOLAE: I hope so. I have ___tried___ to understand, but the United States
(4)
is very different from Romania.

MR. BRASHOV: Don't worry. And thank you for the recipes. I ___have___ not
(5)
___eaten___ any good Romanian food in a long time.
(6)

✪ Put the conversation in order. Number 1 to 4.

_4_ NICOLAE: He's planning to come in tomorrow.

_2_ NICOLAE: Better. He has recovered from the flu.

_3_ KATHERINE: That's good news. When can he come back to work?

_1_ KATHERINE: So, how is Mr. Brashov?

✪✪ Put the conversation in order. Number 1 to 5.

_5_ NICOLAE: I'm sorry, but I have worked very hard to make the café more like home. I thought it would please you.

_1_ NICOLAE: Ah, Victor. Welcome back. We have missed you.

_3_ NICOLAE: But, Victor, they have played for only a short time.

_2_ MR. BRASHOV: Nicolae, what is going on here? Make them stop!

_4_ MR. BRASHOV: I don't care how long they have played! This is not a dance hall. Why have you done this to my café?

✪✪✪ Put the conversation in order. Number 1 to 6.

_5_ ROSA: I have been here for five years and it never feels like home.

_4_ MR. BRASHOV: Not like it? That is not possible. This is the United States. This could have been his home.

_2_ MR. BRASHOV: No, I'm not all right. For a long time I have wanted Nicolae to live in the United States with me. Now he has gone back home to Romania.

_3_ ROSA: Maybe he did not like it here.

_1_ ROSA: Are you all right, Mr. Brashov?

_6_ MR. BRASHOV: Maybe you're right. Maybe Nicolae never felt at home here and the best place for him is Romania. But I will miss him.

In Your Community: Recipes

Nicolae gives this recipe to Mr. Brashov. Answer questions about the recipe. Then tell your answers to someone.

A RECIPE FROM MY KITCHEN. . .

Romanian Noodles With Garlic Sauce

Serves 6

Ingredients
- Medium egg noodles - 1 lb.(pound)
- Olive oil - 5 Tbsp.(tablespoons)
- Garlic - 6 cloves
- Parsley- 3 Tbsp.(tablespoons)
- Basil (dry) - 1/2 tsp.(teaspoon)
- Black pepper - A sprinkle

Method
Noodles
1. Put 8 cups of water in a large pan.
2. Put pan on stove over high heat.
3. Heat water until water begins to boil.
4. Place egg noodles in boiling water.
5. Cook egg noodles for 7-8 minutes.
6. Drain noodles and set them aside.

Sauce
1. Take skin off garlic with a knife.
2. Crush/mash the garlic with a spoon.
3. Put oil in frying pan.
4. Put frying pan over low heat.
5. When oil is hot, put garlic in the pan.
6. When garlic is a little brown, put in parsley and basil. Stir together.
7. Pour mixture of garlic, parsley and basil over hot noodles. Mix together.
8. Put a little black pepper on top of noodles.
9. Serve hot.

✪ 1. What is the name of this dish? _____

2. How many pounds of egg noodles do you need? _____

✪✪ 1. How many ingredients do you need to make this dish? _____

2. What do you do after you cook the noodles? _____

✪✪✪ 1. You have a dinner for ten people. Can you serve this dish as the only food? Tell why or why not.

_____

2. Do you need special things from Romania or is it something Rosa could make in the café? How do you know?

_____

Find two recipes in a newspaper or at home. Try to answer the questions above about your recipes. How are they different from Nicolae's recipe? Do you have the ingredients to make these dishes? What would you need to buy? Tell your answers to someone.

Read and Write: Spotlight on Nicolae

Read the questions. Read Nicolae's postcard very quickly to find the answers. Circle the answers.

✪ What does Nicolae write about?
   a. the news from Romania
   b. his trip on the plane
   c. his feelings about Mr. Brashov and the United States

✪✪ How does Nicolae feel about life in the United States?
   a. He thinks it is different and he likes Romania better.
   b. He doesn't like it because it is too quiet for him here.
   c. He doesn't like the people who live in the United States.

✪✪✪ What is the tone or feeling of this letter?
   a. angry   b. sad   c. worried

Read the postcard again carefully.

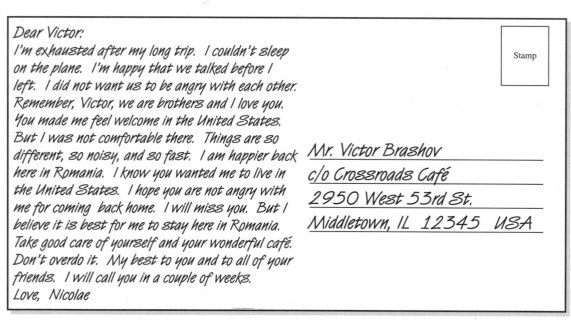

Dear Victor:
I'm exhausted after my long trip. I couldn't sleep
on the plane. I'm happy that we talked before I
left. I did not want us to be angry with each other.
Remember, Victor, we are brothers and I love you.
You made me feel welcome in the United States.
But I was not comfortable there. Things are so
different, so noisy, and so fast. I am happier back
here in Romania. I know you wanted me to live in
the United States. I hope you are not angry with
me for coming back home. I will miss you. But I
believe it is best for me to stay here in Romania.
Take good care of yourself and your wonderful café.
Don't overdo it. My best to you and to all of your
friends. I will call you in a couple of weeks.
Love, Nicolae

Stamp

Mr. Victor Brashov
c/o Crossroads Café
2950 West 53rd St.
Middletown, IL 12345 USA

Find the words in the reading. What do they mean? Circle the answers.

✪ Exhausted:
   a. sad   b. tired   c. happy

✪✪ Nicolae tells Mr. Brashov, "don't overdo it." What does he mean?
   a. Mr. Brashov should work harder at the café.
   b. Mr. Brashov should take a vacation.
   c. Mr. Brashov shouldn't work too hard.

✪✪✪ Nicolae tells Mr. Brashov, "My best to you and all of your friends." What does he mean?
   a. Nicolae sends good wishes to Mr. Brashov and his friends.
   b. Mr. Brashov should treat his friends well.
   c. Mr. Brashov should tell his friends that he got a postcard from Nicolae.

Now you write a postcard about a place you visited. On your postcard include the following information.

✪ 1. the name of the person you are writing to
　 2. the person's address
　 3. the place you visited
　 4. who you went with

✪✪ 1. what you saw on your trip
　　 2. what you did
　　 3. how the weather was
　　 4. how long you stayed

✪✪✪ 1. Tell why you liked or didn't like your trip.
　　　 2. Tell why you would or wouldn't go to this place again.
　　　 3. Tell about your favorite or your worst part of the trip.

	Stamp
	_____
	_____
	_____
	_____

Read your postcard to someone. Then ask: Did you understand? Do you have questions?

What Do You Think?

✪ Why do you think Mr. Brashov is angry at Nicolae? Check (✓) the reasons.

☑ He doesn't like Romanian music.

☑ He is ashamed of Romanian customs.

☐ Nicolae does not understand the way things are in the United States.

☐ He doesn't think that Nicolae can manage the café.

☐ He doesn't want anyone to make changes in the café.

☐ He was sick.

✪✪ Look at the sentences below. Check (✓) I agree, I disagree, or I don't know.

	I agree.	I disagree.	I don't know.
1. Victor, you shouldn't be ashamed of our customs and our language.	☐	☐	☐
2. Sometimes it is hard being away from my family, my friends, and my language.	☐	☐	☐
3. Victor, your life cannot always be work, work, work.	☐	☐	☐

✪✪✪ Answer the questions. Then read your answers to someone.

1. Do you think people should be ashamed of their customs and language? Tell why or why not.

_____

2. Do you think that it is hard being away from one's family, friends, and language? Tell why or why not.

_____

3. Do you think your life should always be work, work, work? Tell why or why not.

_____

Culture Clip: Adjusting to a New Culture

✪ Match.

1. At first, living in a new country can be exciting.

a.

2. At times, newcomers may feel confused when everything around them is moving so fast.

b.

3. People living in new countries sometimes feel very lonely.

c.

4. When newcomers learn more about their new homes, they begin to feel more comfortable.

d.

✪✪ Complete the paragraph about experiences in new countries. Use these words.

comfortable	country	customs	exciting
journey	language	lonely	newcomers

The experience of moving to a new ___country___ can be very _exciting_ at least in the
          (1)   (2)

beginning. When the excitement of the _journey_ begins to fade, some _newcomers_
         (3)   (4)

can get very _lonely_. As they learn more about the _customs_ of the new country
       (5)   (6)

and improve their _language_ skills, they begin to feel more _comfortable_.
        (7)   (8)

✪✪✪ Think.

When people come to new countries to live, they have many different feelings about their experiences. List some of the feelings you experienced when you first came to a new place. What were your experiences? How did you feel at first? How did your feelings change? When did you begin to feel comfortable?

_____

_____

_____

Check Your English

⭐ Write the correct word under each picture.

banner
flag
poster
picture
band ✓
handkerchief ✓

1.
flag

2.
banner

3.
band

4.
poster

5.
picture

6.
handkerchief

⭐⭐ Make a sentence or question from each group of words.

1. fixed   Jamal   stove   has   the

Jamal has fixed the stove. OR _Has Jamal fixed the stove?_

2. have   chess   very   you   well   learned   play   to

You have learned to play chess very well

3. five   been   States   in   has   for   years   Rosa   United   the

Rosa has been in the United States for five Years

4. Nicolae   long   has   Romania   how   in   lived

How long Nicolas has lived in Romania

⭐⭐⭐ Finish the story. Use the words in the box. Write one word in each blank.

Mr. Brashov's brother Nicolae comes from Romania to visit. He __has__ (1)
not seen Mr. Brashov for a long time. Nicolae wants to learn a lot about the
__café__ (2). One day Mr. Brashov becomes __sick__ (3) and has to stay at home.
While Mr. Brashov is sick, Nicolae makes some changes in the café. He makes
changes on the __supply list__ (4) and even has a Romanian __band__ (5) play music.
When Mr. Brashov returns, he becomes __angry__ (6) at Nicolae. He does not like
what Nicolae has __done__ (7). After they talk about this, Nicolae runs from the
café and goes to a __mall__ (8). At the mall, he buys a __gift__ (9) for Mr. Brashov.
He then loses his __wallet__ (10). Nicolae feels lost and alone. He decides to leave
the United States and go back __home__ (11) to Romania. He has __visited__ (12) this
country, but does not want to __stay__ (13). After Nicolae leaves, Mr. Brashov
feels sad because he will miss his brother. ✓

angry
band
bowl of soup
café
changes
done
gift
has
home
live
mall
sick
supply list
stay
visit
visited
wallet

Family Matters

In this unit you will:

- make offers
- read ads for products
- write about a bad decision
- identify problems of single parenting

Ways to Learn

Katherine learns that she can *correct her own mistakes.* She thought she needed more money for her children. She learned that she really needed more time for her children. There are many ways to *correct your own mistakes* in speaking and writing English.

Correct Your Mistakes

Check (✓) the ways you *correct your own mistakes.*

In Conversations

- ☐ use hands and gestures
- ☐ spell or write words
- ☐ repeat words
- ☐ use different words with same meanings
- ☐ other: _____

In Writing

- ☐ use a dictionary
- ☐ apply grammar rules
- ☐ proofread
- ☐ use different words with same meanings
- ☐ other: _____

On Your Own

I can usually find my mistakes in my writing.   YES   NO

I can usually hear my mistakes when speaking.   YES   NO

List ways that help you correct your mistakes:

_____

_____

_____

_____

Before You Watch

Look at the pictures. What do you see?

1.

2.

3.

4.

5.

6.

✪ What do you see in each picture? Write the number of the picture next to the word.

  2   catalogue   _____ TV remote control

_____ drawing   _____ model plane

_____ people hugging   _____ a person yawning

✪✪ What is happening? Write the number of the picture next to the sentence.

  4   Katherine's daughter shows Rosa a drawing.

_____ Katherine and Jamal look at a catalogue.

_____ Katherine's children fight about the TV.

_____ David brings Jess's model airplane to the café.

_____ Jess and Mr. Brashov worry because Katherine is very tired.

_____ Katherine is happy to see her children.

✪✪✪ Write one question you have about each picture. Then read your questions to someone.

1. What is Katherine showing Jamal? _____

2. _____

3. _____

4. _____

5. _____

6. _____

Focus For Watching   Read the questions. Then watch.

✪ 1. Who do the workers at the café worry about?
    2. Who wants to buy a computer?
    3. Who makes a drawing?

✪✪ 1. Who will be fourteen next month?
    2. Who finds out about Katherine's second job?

✪✪✪ 1. Who is supposed to babysit?
    2. Who is left alone?

After You Watch

What do you remember? Match each question with the correct picture. You can use a picture more than once.

★ 1. Who do the workers at the café worry about?

2. Who wants to buy a computer?

3. Who makes a drawing?

a. David

b. Suzanne

★★ 1. Who will be fourteen next month?

2. Who finds out about Katherine's second job?

c. Rosa

★★★ 1. Who is supposed to babysit?

2. Who is left alone?

d. Katherine

★ Read the sentence. Circle Yes or No.

1. Katherine wants to buy a computer for her son. (YES) NO
2. Mr. Brashov gives Katherine a raise. YES NO
3. Suzanne draws a picture of two happy children. YES NO
4. Katherine has two jobs. YES NO

★★ Put the sentences in order. Number 1 to 4.

_____ Rosa finds out Katherine has a second job.

__1__ The people at Crossroads Café worry about Katherine.

_____ Katherine sees Suzanne's drawing.

_____ Katherine takes her children to the lake.

★★★ Write the story. Use the four sentences above. Add these three sentences.
Then close the book and tell the story to someone.

- Katherine finds Suzanne at home without David.
- Katherine is very tired.
- Suzanne draws a picture of two unhappy children.

Katherine is very tired. The people at Crossroads Café worry about Katherine.

_____

_____

_____

_____

_____

_____

_____

_____

_____

_____

_____

Your New Language: Making Offers

I'll help you choose a computer.

To offer to do something for someone else, you can say:

• I'll **help you choose.**

OR

You can ask:

• Would you like me to **help you choose?**

⭐ Complete the conversations. Use these words and phrases.

babysit   fix dinner   help you do it   show you how

1.

I can't dance.

I'll __show you how__.

2.

I'm hungry.

I'll _____.

3.

This homework is hard.

I'll _____.

4.

I need someone to watch Suzanne.

I'll _____.

✪✪ Match.

1. David will be fourteen next month.
2. I'll get you something to eat.
3. Would you like me to teach you to dance?
4. It's cold in here.
5. Is Henry here?

a. I'll get him for you.

b. I'll check the thermostat.

c. Thanks, but I'm not hungry.

d. At fourteen I was working. Would you like me to find him a job?

e. No, thank you. I don't need to learn.

✪✪✪ Complete the conversation. Use these words and phrases. Write one in each blank. You may use a word or phrase more than once.

I'll   Would you like me to

KATHERINE: _Would you like me to_ take you to the lake?
                        (1)

DAVID: Yeah, sure.

KATHERINE: Well, before we go, you'll need to help me around the house.

DAVID: _____ put away the things on the sofa.
                    (2)

SUZANNE: _____ clean off the table.
                    (3)

KATHERINE: Good. But we need to do more than just pick up.

DAVID: _____ take out the garbage, too?
                    (4)

KATHERINE: Yes, David, please do.

SUZANNE: _____ do the dishes.
                    (5)

KATHERINE: And _____ pack the car for the trip.
                        (6)

✪ Put the conversation in order. Number 1 to 3.

___	KATHERINE:	Thank you.
___	JAMAL:	You're right. I'll turn up the heat.
_1_	KATHERINE:	It's too cold in here.

✪✪ Put the conversation in order. Number 1 to 4.

___	KATHERINE:	The house is a mess!
___	DAVID:	What's wrong?
___	KATHERINE:	Good idea. You clean the house and I'll cook dinner.
___	DAVID:	Would you like me to clean it?

✪✪✪ Put the conversation in order. Number 1 to 6.

___	JAMAL:	Would you like me to look at it?
___	JAMAL:	What kind of trouble?
___	JAMAL:	I hope we don't have to do that. They're expensive.
___	MR. BRASHOV:	I'm having trouble with the thermostat.
___	MR. BRASHOV:	Please. And then if you can't fix it, I'll call a repair person.
___	MR. BRASHOV:	I can't get the on/off switch to move.

In Your Community: Product Advertisements

These are advertisements from the catalogue that Katherine showed Jamal. Answer the questions about the ads. Then share your answers with someone.

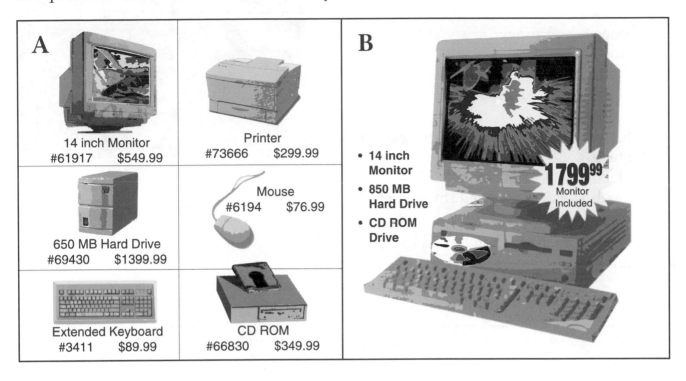

A

14 inch Monitor
#61917 $549.99

Printer
#73666 $299.99

650 MB Hard Drive
#69430 $1399.99

Mouse
#6194 $76.99

Extended Keyboard
#3411 $89.99

CD ROM
#66830 $349.99

B

- **14 inch Monitor**
- **850 MB Hard Drive**
- **CD ROM Drive**

1799⁹⁹
Monitor Included

✪ 1. What is the order number (#) of the monitor in ad A? _____

2. What is the price of the computer system in ad B? _____

✪✪ 1. What is the total cost of the components shown in ad A?

_____

2. What is the difference between the two hard drives?

_____

✪✪✪ 1. Compare ads A and B. What component isn't included in ad B?

_____

2. Is it cheaper to buy the components separately or to buy the complete system? How much is the price difference?

_____

Find an ad in a newspaper, store catalogue, or mail order catalogue from your community. How is it the same as or different from the one above?

Read and Write: Spotlight on Katherine

Read the questions. Read Katherine's diary entry
very quickly to find the answers. Circle the answers.

✪ What does Katherine write about?
   a. her job at the café
   b. her son's school
   c. problems with her second job

✪✪ How does Katherine feel about the second job?
   a. She feels good about it.
   b. She feels it was a mistake.
   c. She feels she doesn't need the money.

✪✪✪ What is the tone or feeling of this letter?
   a. regret   b. anticipation   c. joy

Read the diary entry again carefully.

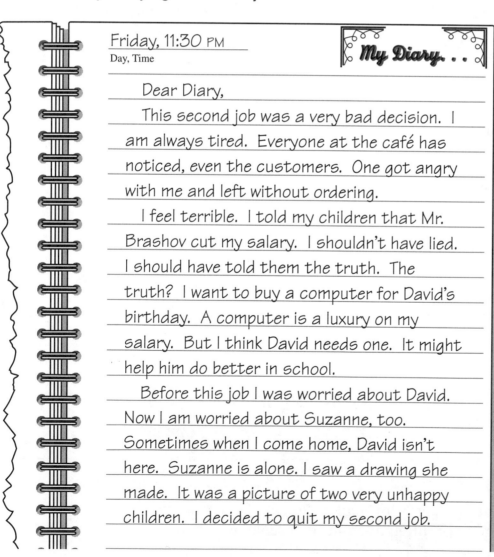

Friday, 11:30 PM
Day, Time

My Diary. . .

   Dear Diary,
   This second job was a very bad decision. I
am always tired. Everyone at the café has
noticed, even the customers. One got angry
with me and left without ordering.
   I feel terrible. I told my children that Mr.
Brashov cut my salary. I shouldn't have lied.
I should have told them the truth. The
truth? I want to buy a computer for David's
birthday. A computer is a luxury on my
salary. But I think David needs one. It might
help him do better in school.
   Before this job I was worried about David.
Now I am worried about Suzanne, too.
Sometimes when I come home, David isn't
here. Suzanne is alone. I saw a drawing she
made. It was a picture of two very unhappy
children. I decided to quit my second job.

Find the words in the
reading that mean the
same as the phrases
below. Write the correct
word below each phrase.

✪ not tell the truth

_____

✪✪ a picture

_____

✪✪✪ something you
don't need

_____

Now you write a diary entry about a decision you made that you think was a mistake. Give the following information.

⭐ What was the decision?
When did you make it?

⭐⭐ What happened?
Why was it a bad decision?

⭐⭐⭐ What did you do when you realized it was a bad decision?
Based on your experience, what advice would you give a friend?

Read your entry to someone. Then ask: Did you understand? Do you have questions?

What Do You Think?

✪ Katherine wants to buy David a computer for his birthday, but she doesn't have enough money. What should she do? Check one.

☐ She should buy him something else.

☐ She should work more to make more money.

☐ She should tell David the problem.

✪✪ Look at the sentences below. Check (✓) I agree, I disagree, or I don't know.

	I agree.	I disagree.	I don't know.
1. When something is wrong, everybody is affected.	☐	☐	☐
2. My children need me more than they need expensive presents.	☐	☐	☐
3. A parent's work is never done.	☐	☐	☐

✪✪✪ Answer the questions. Then read your answers to someone.

1. Do you think everybody is affected when something is wrong with one person? Tell why or why not.

_____

2. Do you think spending time with children is more important than buying them things? Tell why or why not.

_____

3. Do you think a parent's work is ever done? Tell why or why not.

_____

Culture Clip: Single Parenting

⭐ Match.

1. Single parents need to work outside their homes.

2. They also have work to do at home.

3. They need to spend free time with their children.

4. When children are alone, they feel sad.

a.

b.

c.

d.

⭐⭐ Complete the sentences. Write one word in each blank. Use these words.

children	earn	financial	pulled
concern	families	hard	separated

One out of every four __families__ in the United States is a single-parent family. Money
(1)
is a big _____. It is not easy to provide _____ support for their families and
(2)   (3)
nurture their _____. They feel _____ in many directions. Sometimes in
(4)   (5)
order to _____ money to support children, single parents have to be _____
(6)   (7)
from their chidren. That is _____ for both parents and children.
(8)

⭐⭐⭐ David is angry with his mother because she is never home. He tells her "Go back to Dad." Do you think it is important for children to have two parents? Why or why not? Write your ideas. Then tell your ideas to someone.

_____

_____

Check Your English

✪ Write the correct word under each picture.

catalogue

drawing

people
  hugging

TV remote
  control

model airplane

a person
  yawning

1.

2.

3.

4.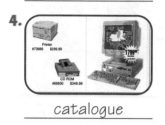
catalogue

5.

6.

✪✪ Make a sentence or question from each group of words.

1. dance   teach   I'll   you   to

   I'll teach you to dance.

2. you   help   homework   your   with   I'll

   _____

3. would   letters   mail   you   to   me   like   your

   _____

4. you   to   you   like   help   would   me   decorate

   _____

✪✪✪ Finish the story. Use the words in the box. Write one word in each blank.

Katherine wants to give her son, David, a __computer__ for his birthday.
                                              (1)
Computers are expensive. She needs extra _____, so she gets a second
                                              (2)
job. It causes _____. The workers at Crossroads Café _____ about
                  (3)   (4)
Katherine because she is always _____.
                                     (5)

  Katherine gets home from work _____ every night. David is unhappy.
                                     (6)
He has to _____ his little sister, Suzanne, so he can't see his _____.
              (7)   (8)
David doesn't do his _____, so he and his mother argue. He wants his
                         (9)
mother and father to be _____.
                            (10)

  Katherine sees her daughter's _____ of two unhappy children. She
                                    (11)
decides time with her children is _____ important than money.
                                      (12)

| |
| alone |
| babysit |
| computer |
| drawing |
| early |
| friends |
| homework |
| late |
| less |
| money |
| more |
| problems |
| tired |
| together |
| worry |

Rush to Judgment

In this unit you will:

- describe people
- read a police report
- write a letter requesting information
- describe the roles of the police

Ways to Learn

Jamal has to *guess* why the police stopped him. Do they think he did something wrong? Do they want to help him? Sometimes *guessing* helps you understand meanings.

Guess English Meanings

When do you *guess* English meaning in reading and speaking? Fill in the blank with 1, 2, or 3.

1 = often   2 = sometimes   3 = never

Reading
___ look for word endings (ing, ed, es)
___ look for similar words in my language
___ read the whole sentence
___ look for where the word is used (signs, envelopes, etc.)

Speaking
___ look for gestures, hand movements
___ look for facial expressions
___ listen to whole conversation, then guess about meaning
___ listen for tone of voice

On Your Own

I am a good *guesser.*   YES   NO
Guessing helps me.   YES   NO

The last time I *guessed* about English meaning . . . (circle one)

I was right. I was wrong.   I learned something.

Before You Watch

Look at the pictures. What do you see?

1.

2.

3.

4.

5.

6.

✪ What do you see in each picture? Write the number of the picture next to the word.

_3_ patrol car   ___ license plate

___ toolbox   ___ police officer

___ handcuffs   ___ police station

✪✪ What is happening? Write the number of the picture next to the sentence.

_5_ Jamal has handcuffs on his wrists.

___ There are two men in a car.

___ Mr. Brashov walks out of the police station with Jamal.

___ Jamal picks up his tools.

___ Two men talk to Mr. Brashov.

___ A man pushes Jamal against the car.

✪✪✪ Write one question you have about each picture. Then read your questions to someone.

1. What is the man doing to Jamal? _____

2. _____

3. _____

4. _____

5. _____

6. _____

Focus For Watching   Read the questions. Then watch.

✪ 1. Who has a problem on his way to work?
2. Who is Henry looking for?
3. Who asks Jamal a lot of questions?

✪✪ 1. Who welcomes the police to the neighborhood?
2. Who does Jamal call for help?
3. Who gets angry with Henry?

✪✪✪ 1. Who brings Henry's grandparents to the café?
2. Who do the police try to contact about Jamal?

After You Watch

What do you remember? Match each question with the correct picture. You can use a picture more than once.

 1. Who has a problem on his way to work?

2. Who is Henry looking for?

3. Who asks Jamal a lot of questions?

 1. Who welcomes the police to the neighborhood?

2. Who does Jamal call for help?

3. Who gets angry with Henry?

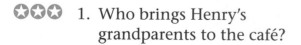 1. Who brings Henry's grandparents to the café?

2. Who do the police try to contact about Jamal?

a. Mr. Brashov

b. Officers Benton and Anderson

c. Grandma and Grandpa Chang

d. Jamal

e. Officer Kang

f. Mrs. Chang

g. Jihan

✪ Read the sentences. Circle Yes or No.
1. The police take Jamal to Crossroads Café. YES (NO)
2. Jamal has to answer questions at the police station. YES NO
3. The police watch Jamal as he picks up his tools on the street. YES NO
4. Jamal calls his wife for help. YES NO

✪✪ Put the sentences in order. Number 1 to 4.

_____ Mr. Brashov comes to the police station to help Jamal.

__1__ The police see Jamal on the street with his toolbox.

_____ The police do not believe Jamal and take him to the police station in handcuffs.

_____ The officers finally believe Jamal and tell him that he can leave.

✪✪✪ Write the story. Use the four sentences above. Add these three sentences.
Then close the book and tell the story to someone.
- Jamal has to answer many questions at the police station.
- The officers want to know why Jamal has a lot of tools.
- Jamal makes a phone call to Crossroads Café to ask for help.

The police see Jamal on the street with his toolbox. The officers want to know why Jamal
has a lot of tools.

_____

_____

_____

_____

_____

_____

_____

_____

_____

_____

_____

Your New Language: Describing people

> The suspect is in his late twenties with a medium build.

To describe people, you can say:

- He is a **short** man.
- Jamal is a **valued employee**.
- He is **in** his early fifties.

⭐ Complete the conversations. Use these words.

innocent   bad   missing   brown hair   gray

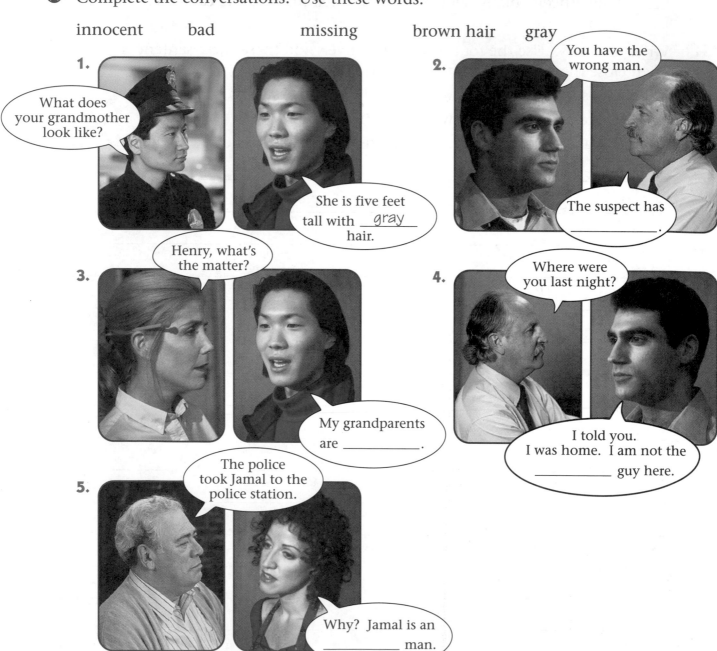

1.

> What does your grandmother look like?

> She is five feet tall with ___gray___ hair.

2.

> You have the wrong man.

> The suspect has _____.

3.

> Henry, what's the matter?

> My grandparents are _____.

4.

> Where were you last night?

> I told you. I was home. I am not the _____ guy here.

5.

> The police took Jamal to the police station.

> Why? Jamal is an _____ man.

✪✪ Match.

1. How tall is your
   grandmother?

2. How old is the
   customer?

3. Is the man heavy?

4. Why is Jamal at the
   police station?

5. What kind of hair does
   she have?

a. It is short and blond.

b. She is about five feet tall.

c. The police think he is guilty.

d. She is in her early forties.

e. No. He has a medium build.

✪✪✪ Complete the conversation. Use these words. Write one in each blank. You
may use a word more than once.

tired	twenties	suspect	sick
medium build	dark hair	innocent	wrong

ANDERSON: Can I see some identification?

JAMAL: Yes, . . . oh, where is . . . I was so ____tired____ this morning I forgot
(1)
my wallet.

ANDERSON: What's your name?

JAMAL: Jamal Al Jibali.

ANDERSON: Where were you last night?

JAMAL: I was at home. My daughter was _____. Is there a problem here?
(2)

ANDERSON: It says here that the _____ is a male in his _____. He has
(3)   (4)

_____ and a _____.
(5)   (6)

JAMAL: O.K. I look like that. But I am _____. You have the
(7)

_____ man.
(8)

✪ Put the conversation in order. Number 1 to 4.

___	BENTON:	No, she is with a white male in his mid thirties.
___	ANDERSON:	Is she alone?
___	BENTON:	She is tall with long, brown hair.
1	ANDERSON:	What does our suspect look like?

✪✪ Put the conversation in order. Number 1 to 6.

___	JESS:	Don't worry, Henry, we'll find them. What do they look like?
___	JESS:	How about your grandfather?
___	HENRY:	O.K. My grandmother is five feet tall with gray hair.
___	HENRY:	My grandparents are missing.
___	JESS:	Let's go look for them. I'll give you a ride in my car.
___	HENRY:	His hair is a little gray, too. He is about five feet five inches tall, has a slim build, and wears glasses.

✪✪✪ Put the conversation in order. Number 1 to 7.

___	JESS:	There is something about burglaries here in the newspaper. The suspect is a male in his late twenties with a medium build and short dark hair.
___	MR. BRASHOV:	To question him. Something about some burglaries.
___	MR. BRASHOV:	That sounds like a description of Jamal, doesn't it?
___	MR. BRASHOV:	The police took Jamal to the police station.
___	MR. BRASHOV:	I hope the police know it, too.
___	JESS:	Yes, it does. But I know Jamal wasn't involved in any of this.
___	JESS:	Why?

In Your Community: Police Report

The police filled out a report about Jamal. Answer the questions about the report. Then tell your answers to someone.

1. DATE: 12/17		
2. NAME: (LAST) Al-Jibali	3. (FIRST): Jamal	4. MIDDLE INITIAL: N
5. GENDER: Male	6. DATE OF BIRTH (D.O.B.): 12/15/65	
7. DRIVER'S LICENSE #: N/A	8. WEAPONS? NO	
9. HEIGHT: 5 ft. 7 in.	10. WEIGHT: 150 lbs.	11. HAIR: brown-short
12. BUILD: medium	13. EYES: brown	
14. MARKS: 1 scar—left hand near thumb		
15. GLASSES: Yes	16. COMPLEXION: medium	
17. HOME ADDRESS: 17 Cummings St. Apt #2, Middletown		
18. PHONE NUMBER: 555-6279		
19. MARITAL STATUS: Married		
20. NAME OF SPOUSE: (LAST) El-Bially	21. (FIRST): Jihan	
22. PLACE OF EMPLOYMENT: Crossroads Café		
23. ADDRESS: 2950 West 53rd St., Middletown		
24. PHONE NUMBER: 555-2345		
25. NAME OF EMPLOYER: Mr. Victor Brashov		
26. PERSON TO CONTACT IN CASE OF EMERGENCY: Mrs. Jihan El-Bially		
27. OCCUPATION: Engineer		
28. PLACE OF BIRTH: Cairo, Egypt	29. U.S. CITIZEN? No	
30. PERMANENT RESIDENT? Yes		

Description of incident: We saw the subject, Mr. Jamal Al-Jibali on the street with a box full of tools. He fit the description of a suspect involved in a series of burglaries in our area. When we questioned Mr. Al-Jibali, he didn't have any I.D. He could not prove where he was last night. We took Mr. Al-Jibali to the police station to answer a few questions. Later he was released.

Signature: _Detective Benton_

✪ 1. Where does Jamal live? __17 Cummings St. Apt. #2, Middletown__

2. How much does Jamal weigh? _____

3. What is his wife's last name? _____

4. How tall is he? _____

✪✪ Read Detective Benton's report again. Answer the questions about the report.
1. Did Jamal have a gun when the police searched him? How do you know?

_____

2. Has Jamal lived his entire life in the United States? How do you know?

_____

✪✪✪ 1. According to the report, Jamal was taken to the police station for questioning because he looked like the suspect. If the burglar was very large with blond hair, would Jamal have fit the description? Why or why not?

_____

2. This report contains some information that is not true. Find the mistake in the report. Tell how you know it is a mistake.

_____

Find a missing person's poster, a wanted poster, or a crime story in your newspaper. Try to find all of the information that is here in Jamal's report. Tell your answers to someone.

Read and Write: Spotlight on Jamal

Read the questions. Read Jamal's letter very quickly to find the answers. Circle the answers.

✪ What does Jamal write about?
a. problems at the café
b. his problem with the police
c. his work as a handyman

✪✪ How does Jamal feel about the police?
a. angry
b. worried
c. happy

✪✪✪ What is the tone or feeling of this letter?
a. sad   b. funny   c. serious

Read the letter again carefully.

Find the words in the reading. What do they mean? Circle the answers.

✪ Legal means:
a. something about the law
b. something about the restaurant
c. something about repairs

✪✪ A lawyer is a person who:
a. takes care of your health
b. helps you understand the law
c. fills out forms for the police

✪✪✪ A pamphlet is:
a. a large book
b. a little book
c. a small advertisement in a newspaper

Crossroads Café
2950 West 53rd St.
Middletown, IL 12345

Center for Legal Rights
1257 Main Street - Suite 620
Middletown, IL 12345

Dear Sir/Madam:

   I would like to get some information about my legal rights and the rights of the police. Last week I had an experience with the police in my community. They took me to the police station and asked me a lot of questions. I didn't even know why I was there.

   I didn't have a lawyer with me and I felt angry and scared. I don't think that the police were right. But I am not sure about the things they can do.

   Please send me your pamphlet, *Know Your Rights* so I can learn more about my legal rights. I want to know these things in case this ever happens to me again.

   Thank you. I hope to receive this information soon. If you want to contact me, please call 555-6279.

Sincerely yours,

Jamal Al-Jibali
Jamal Al-Jibali

Now you write a letter to request information. In your letter, include the following information.

✪ 1. the name of the person you are writing to
  2. the address of the person
  3. what you want the person to do (to call, send you something, etc.)

✪✪ 1. the information you want
  2. why you want this information
  3. what you are going to do with the information

✪✪✪ 1. thank the person for helping you
  2. include information so the person can contact you

What Do You Think?

✪ Why do the police take Jamal to the police station? Check (✓) the reasons.

☐ because he was involved in a burglary

☐ because he looked like the burglary suspect

☐ because he had tools on the street

☐ because he is from another country

☐ because he did not have any identification with him

☐ other: _____

✪✪ Look at the sentences below. Check (✓) I agree, I disagree, or I don't know.

		I agree.	I disagree.	I don't know.
1.	I should call a lawyer for my friend.	☐	☐	☐
2.	You are not allowed to keep Jamal here like this.	☐	☐	☐
3.	From what I hear, the police here aren't very nice.	☐	☐	☐

✪✪✪ Answer the questions. Then read your answers to someone.

1. Do you think Mr. Brashov should call a lawyer for Jamal?
   Tell why or why not.

   _____

2. Do you think the police are allowed to keep Jamal at the police station?
   Tell why or why not.

   _____

3. Do you think the police are nice in this country? Tell why or why not.

   _____

Culture Clip: Roles of a Police Officer

⭐ Match.

1. Police officers often work with children in the community.

a.

2. It is good for a police officer to be able to speak another language to get information from community members.

b.

3. It is important that a police officer be known by name in the community.

c.

⭐⭐ Complete the paragraph about the roles of the police officer. Use these words.

arresting	children	community	crime
friends	happening	jail	merchants
police officer	public	tickets	

Officer Garcia says, "I became a police officer because I like to work with the __public__. It is
(1)
important that we find time to work with young _____ in the _____ in a positive way.
(2) (3)
We also try to be _____ with the _____ in the community. The merchants help us
(4) (5)
know what is _____ in the area. Many people feel that our main job involves _____
(6) (7)
people and writing _____. In fact, many of us prefer to work to prevent _____. We
(8) (9)
don't want to take people to _____. I enjoy my job more when the community treats me as
(10)
a person with a name, rather than as only a _____.
(11)

⭐⭐⭐ Think.

Jamal was stopped by the police. Do you think those police officers would agree with Officer Garcia about the roles of a police officer? Why or why not?

_____

_____

Check Your English

✪ Write the correct word under each picture.

license plate

patrol car

police station

handcuffs

toolbox

police officer

1.

license plate

2.

_____

3.

_____

4.

_____

5.

_____

6.

_____

✪✪ Make a sentence or question from each group of words.

1. man   is   Jamal   an   innocent

   Jamal is an innocent man. OR Is Jamal an innocent man?

2. like   what   man   does   look   the

   _____

3. mid   suspect   a   the   tall   his   twenties   man   is   in

   _____

4. customer   long   eyes   and   hair   has   blue   the   dark   big

   _____

✪✪✪ Finish the story. Use the words in the box. Write one word in each blank.

Jamal is on his way to work. Two _police officers_ see him drop his _____.
                                        (1)   (2)

They ask Jamal why he has a lot of tools. He says he needs the _____
                                                                      (3)

for his work. The police don't think Jamal is telling the _____ so they
                                                                (4)

put _____ on him. They take him to the _____. At the station,
       (5)   (6)

Jamal has to answer many _____. Jamal makes a phone call to
                              (7)

Crossroads Café to ask for _____. Mr. Brashov comes to the police station
                               (8)

to find out about Jamal. The officers _____ believe Jamal's story and tell
                                            (9)

him that he can leave. Jamal is _____ because of the way the police
                                     (10)

treated him. But he is _____ that the day is over. He wants to learn
                            (11)

more about his _____ rights and the _____ of the police. So he
                   (12)   (13)

writes a letter to get information.

angry
detective
finally
glad
handcuffs
help
late twenties
legal
police officers
police station
questions
rights
suspect
toolbox
tools
truth

10 Let the Buyer Beware

In this unit you will:

- give compliments
- respond to compliments
- read advertisements for services
- write a newspaper article
- identify scams

Ways to Learn

Mr. Brashov *reflects on what he learned* after he finds out about Barbara's plan. He *thinks about what he learned* and *asks himself how he learned.*

Reflect on Learning

Circle what you know about how you learn language.

1. I learn better if I study . . .
   a. at home
   b. at school
   c. at the library
2. I need to practice my new language . . .
   a. right away
   b. tomorrow
   c. next week
3. I like to learn new vocabulary by . . .
   a. writing words
   b. memorizing words
   c. using words in conversation

4. The most important part of language learning for me is . . .
   a. reading
   b. conversation
   c. grammar
   d. pronunciation

On Your Own

After you complete Unit 10 worktext, complete the following sentences.

1. The most helpful exercise for me was _____ because _____
2. The most difficult exercise for me was _____ because _____
3. I can remember the new language in Unit 10 if I _____

Before You Watch

Look at the pictures. What do you see?

1.

2.

3.

4.

5.

6.

✪ What do you see in each picture? Write the number of the picture next to the word.

_____ people arguing   _____ photo

_____ check   _____ money

_____ dessert   _1_ order pad

✪✪ What is happening? Write the number of the picture next to the sentence.

_____ Mr. Brashov and the woman go out to dinner.

_____ The woman gives Mr. Brashov some money.

_1_ Katherine waits on a new customer.

_____ Jamal and Katherine show Mr. Brashov a photo.

_____ The woman and Mr. Brashov argue about the check.

_____ The waiter hands something to Katherine.

✪✪✪ Write one question you have about each picture. Then read your questions to someone.

1. _____

2. _____

3. _____

4. _____

5. _____

6. _____

Focus For Watching   Read the questions. Then watch.

✪ 1. Who makes a date with Mr. Brashov?
   2. Who gives Barbara money?
   3. Who gives Mr. Brashov $800?

✪✪ 1. Who sees Barbara with another man?
   2. Who takes pictures of Barbara?

✪✪✪ 1. Who loans Mr. Brashov the award?
   2. Who gives Mr. Brashov checks for $800?

After You Watch

What do you remember? Match each question with the correct picture. You can use an answer more than once.

★ 1. Who makes a date with Mr. Brashov?

a. Bill

2. Who gives Barbara money?

b. Mr. Brashov

3. Who gives Mr. Brashov $800?

c. Barbara

★★ 1. Who sees Barbara with another man?

d. Jamal

2. Who takes pictures of Barbara?

e. Jess

★★★ 1. Who loans Mr. Brashov the award?

2. Who gives Mr. Brashov checks for $800?

f. Katherine

★ Read the sentences. Circle Yes or No.

1. Barbara wants Mr. Brashov's money.   (YES)   NO
2. Mr. Brashov gives Barbara some money.   YES   NO
3. Mr. Brashov and his friends trick Barbara.   YES   NO
4. Mr. Brashov gets his money back.   YES   NO

★★ Put the sentences in order. Number 1 to 4.

_____   Barbara tells Mr. Brashov she'll make Crossroads Café famous.

_____   Mr. Brashov gets his money back.

__1__   Mr. Brashov worries because business is slow.

_____   Mr. Brashov gives Barbara $800.

★★★ Write the story. Use the four sentences above. Add these three sentences.
Then close your book and tell the story to someone.

• Mr. Brashov and Barbara make a date.
• Barbara sees Jess and Bill hand checks to Mr. Brashov.
• Jamal takes pictures of Barbara with another man.

Mr. Brashov worries because business is slow. Mr. Brashov and Barbara make a date.

_____

_____

_____

_____

_____

_____

_____

_____

_____

_____

_____

_____

Your New Language: Giving Compliments

> I'm sure you'll be very successful, Victor. You're a very charming man.

> Thank you.

To give compliments you can say:

- You **are charming.**
- Your restaurant **is charming.**
- You **are very charming.**
- Your restaurant **is very charming.**
- You are a **very charming man.**
- Your restaurant is a **very charming place.**

⭐ Complete the conversations. Use these words.

delicious   smart   friendly   wonderful

1.

> This apple strudel is <u>delicious</u>.

> Thank you.

2.

> Crossroads Café is a _____ place.

> Thank you.

3.

> I can make Crossroads Café famous.

> That's a _____ idea.

4.

> Victor, you are a _____ man.

> Thank you.

✪✪ Match.

1. Crossroads Café is an interesting name.
2. You are a very skilled chess player.
3. You are a very serious student.
4. The service here is superb and the food is magnificent.
5. This apple strudel is delicious.

a. I'm glad you like it. It was my wife's recipe.
b. Thank you. I think my studies will help me get a good job.
c. I think so, too. Jess, one of my regular customers, named it.
d. Thank you. I was the school champion.
e. Thank you. We received an award as one of the top ten restaurants in the city.

✪✪✪ Complete the conversation. Use these sentences.

The judges were very generous.
The chef is very skilled.
The waitstaff works very hard.

BARBARA: The food here is great.

BILL'S FATHER: I think so, too. ___The chef is very skilled.___
                                        (1)

BARBARA: And your service is the best.

BILL'S FATHER: Thank you. _____
                                (2)

BARBARA: I understand you won the award as the number one restaurant in the city.

BILL'S FATHER: Yes. _____
                          (3)

✪ Put the conversation in order. Number 1 to 3.

_____ KATHERINE: Thank you. I'll tell the chef.

__1__ KATHERINE: How is everything?

_____ CUSTOMER: Fine. The chicken is very good.

✪✪ Put the conversation in order. Number 1 to 4.

_____ PERSON #1: Wow! You must be a very good seamstress.

_____ PERSON #1: I really like your dress.

_____ PERSON #2: Thanks. I made it myself.

_____ PERSON #2: I'm O.K., I guess. Actually, it was pretty easy to make.

✪✪✪ Put the conversation in order. Number 1 to 7.

_____ COACH: I'm sorry to hear that.

_____ COACH: Really? I thought he was already good.

_____ COACH: Well, I think he's great, too!

_____ FATHER: Thank you. He's improved a lot since you became his coach.

_____ COACH: Your son is an excellent baseball player.

_____ FATHER: But he is fine, now. He thinks you're great.

_____ FATHER: Well, he didn't like his last coach, so he didn't do his best for him.

In Your Community: Advertisements

Barbara tells Victor she can make his restaurant famous. Actually, she is a con artist—she takes $800 from Victor, but she doesn't plan to promote his restaurant.

Sometimes con artists advertise in a newspaper or magazine. Answer the questions about these ads. Then tell your answers to someone.

#1.
> Become a Certified
> **TRAVEL AGENT**
> Enjoy discounted travel.
> Operate from home or
> office. Earn substantial
> income. ONLY $199
> 1-800-555-3600, Ext. 13

#2.
> 1-800-555-2112
> **FREE LAS VEGAS
> VACATION**
> and a lifetime of income
> & travel discounts with
> the purchase of our
> home-based travel
> agency for $495

✪ 1. What does ad #1 promise? _____

2. How much money does it ask for? _____

3. What does ad #2 promise? _____

4. How much money does it ask for? _____

✪✪ 1. In ad #1, what is too good to be true?

_____

_____

2. In ad #2, what is too good to be true?

_____

_____

✪✪✪ Write one question you would ask for each ad if you called about each ad.

1. _____

_____

2. _____

_____

Now look in a newspaper or magazine for an ad that offers a service or product, but asks for money. How is the ad the same as or different from the ads above?

Read and Write: Spotlight on Henry

Read the questions. Read Henry's story from his school newspaper very quickly to find the answers. Circle the answers.

★ Who is the story about?
a. Barbara and Mr. Brashov
b. Katherine and Bill
c. Jess and Bill

★★ How does Mr. Brashov feel about Barbara?
a. sad she is not good looking
b. surprised she is interested in him
c. disappointed she isn't interested in him

★★★ What is the tone or feeling of the story?
a. thoughtful   b. amusing   c. cheerful

Read the newspaper article again carefully.

THE NEIGHBORHOOD BEAT
by Henry Chang

There was some excitement at Crossroads Café this month. A woman named Barbara came into the café one day. Barbara made a date with the owner, Victor Brashov. Mr. Brashov couldn't believe that she was interested in him.

They went out to dinner. Barbara told Mr. Brashov that she could make Crossroads Café famous. Mr. Brashov gave her $800 to promote Crossroads Café.

A few days later, the café waitress saw Barbara with another man. She saw the man give Barbara a check. Barbara uses her charm and good looks to take money from lonely men.

The moral? Be careful of something that is too good to be true.

Find the word in the reading. What does it mean? Circle the answer.

★ promote
a. buy   b. make bigger   c. help make famous

★★ moral
a. goodness   b. lesson   c. story

★★★ charm
a. good looks   b. money   c. nice personality

Now you add to Henry's article. Answer these questions.

✪ Tell more about Barbara. How old is she? Is she attractive? How does she dress?

✪✪ Why does Mr. Brashov trust Barbara enough to give her money?

✪✪✪ How does Mr. Brashov get his money back?

Read your article to someone. Then ask: Did you understand? Do you have questions?

What Do You Think?

✪ Why do you think Barbara decided to take money from Mr. Brashov?
Check (✓) the reasons. You may check more than one.

☐ because he is a fool

☐ because he is trusting

☐ because he is from another country

☐ because he speaks with an accent

☐ other

✪✪ Look at the sentences below. Check (✓) I agree, I disagree, or I don't know.

	I agree.	I disagree.	I don't know.
1. In this country you can invest one dollar and make one million.	☐	☐	☐
2. The world is full of con artists.	☐	☐	☐
3. Con artists think they can take advantage of anyone who is from another country or speaks with an accent.	☐	☐	☐

✪✪✪ Answer the questions. Then read your answers to someone.

1. Do you think you can invest one dollar and make one million?
Tell why or why not.

_____

2. Do you think the world is full of con artists? Tell why or why not.

_____

3. Do you think con artists take advantage of only people who come from
another country? Tell why or why not.

_____

Culture Clip: Consumer Scams

⭐ Match

1. She wants to sell a used car.

a.

2. He sells products from door to door.

b.

3. He tells people they won a contest and then asks for money.

c.

⭐⭐ Complete the sentences. Write one word in each blank. Use these words.

businesses	information	sell	careful
product	selling	complain	salespeople

There are times when buyers must be very careful. Be careful of

__salespeople__ who pressure you. Be careful of people who _____ things
   (1)   (2)

from door to door. Be _____ of people who sell things over the
                       (3)

telephone. If you have questions about a _____ or the people who are
                                           (4)

_____ it, call the Better Business Bureau. They keep records of
  (5)

_____ that people _____ about. They will share this _____
  (6)   (7)   (8)

with you. If a bargain sounds too good to be true, it generally is.

⭐⭐⭐ Barbara promised to help promote Crossroads Café. Do you think
Mr. Brashov should have guessed she was a con artist? Write your ideas.
Then tell your ideas to someone.

_____

_____

_____

_____

Check Your English

✪ Write the correct word under each picture.

check
dessert
order pad
photo
money
people arguing

1.   2.   3.   4.   5.   6.

check _____ _____ _____ _____ _____

✪✪ Make a compliment from each group of words.

1. dessert   delicious   is   this

   This dessert is delicious.

2. man   trusting   are   you   a

   _____

3. a   Café   charming   very   Crossroads   is   place

   _____

4. skilled   a   Jamal   are   engineer   very   you

   _____

✪✪✪ Finish the story. Use the words in the box. Write one word in each blank.

Business is slow. Victor is __worried__ . Then Barbara comes into the café.
                  (1)
She is very attractive, and she makes a _____ with Victor. They go to
                                  (2)
Palmettos Restaurant for dinner. Barbara tells Mr. Brashov that she helps
restaurant owners _____ . She can make Crossroads Café _____ .
                  (3)   (4)
Mr. Brashov gives her $800 to _____ Crossroads Café.
                                 (5)

A few days later Katherine is at Palmettos with Bill, the son of the
_____ . Katherine sees Barbara there with another man. She begins to
(6)
_____ about Mr. Brashov. Bill arranges for Jamal to be a waiter. Jamal
(7)
_____ photos of the man giving Barbara a _____ . They show the
(8)   (9)
_____ to Mr. Brashov. Mr. Brashov decides that Barbara isn't _____
(10)   (11)
in him. She is only interested in his _____ .
                                 (12)
When Barbara comes back to the café for another $800, Mr. Brashov tricks
her. He _____ her a share in his café for $800.
      (13)

advertise
check
date
famous
interested
makes
money
owner
photos
promote
promoter
rich
sells
takes
worried
worry

11 No Vacancy

In this unit you will:

- ask for clarification
- read a rental application
- write about discrimination
- identify causes of discrimination

Ways to Learn

Rosa has a problem with her apartment. She *asks for help* from her friends. *Asking others for help* is an important part of learning.

Ask For Help

Check (✓) ways you *ask for help*.

- [ ] I ask someone who knows the answer.
- [ ] I tell why I need help.
- [ ] I have a clear, specific question.
- [ ] I am not afraid to ask.
- [ ] I ask twice if needed.
- [ ] I say, "Excuse me." and "Please."
- [ ] other: _____

On Your Own

Tell how you *asked for help* with English last week.

Who did you ask?   **What question did you ask?**

_____   _____

_____   _____

Asking for help is difficult for me.   YES   NO
I will *ask for help* more often.   YES   NO

Before You Watch

Look at the pictures. What do you see?

1.

2.

3.

4.

5.

6.

✪ What do you see in each picture? Write the number of the picture next to the word.

_3_   an excited person   _____ tape measure

_____ a big smile   _____ video camera

_____ a person pointing   _____ videotape

✪✪ What is happening? Write the number of the picture next to the sentence.

_4_   The apartment manager shows the apartment to a man and a young woman.

_____ Jamal measures a room.

_____ Rosa looks at an apartment.

_____ Jamal helps Henry with a video camera.

_____ Rosa receives a phone call.

_____ Henry shows the manager his videotape.

✪✪✪ Write one question you have about each picture. Then read your questions to someone.

1. What is Jamal reading? _____

2. _____

3. _____

4. _____

5. _____

6. _____

Focus For Watching   Read the questions. Then watch.

✪ 1. Who is looking for a new apartment?
   2. Who is the apartment manager?
   3. Who videotapes people looking at the apartment?

✪✪ 1. Who sees the manager showing the apartment?
    2. To whom does the manager want to rent the apartment?
    3. Who finds out about discrimination laws?

✪✪✪ 1. Who thinks Rosa is being discriminated against?
     2. Who has an idea to prove discrimination?
     3. Who says "I don't like the view?"

After You Watch

What do you remember? Match each question with the correct picture. You can use a picture more than once.

⭐ 1. Who looks for a new apartment?

2. Who is the property manager?

3. Who videotapes people looking at the apartment?

⭐⭐ 1. Who sees the manager showing the apartment?

2. To whom does the apartment manager want to rent the apartment?

3. Who finds out about the laws on discrimination?

⭐⭐⭐ 1. Who thinks Rosa is being discriminated against?

2. Who has an idea for proving discrimination?

3. Who says "I don't like the view?"

a. Jess

b. Rosa

c. Dorothy Walsh

d. Patty Peterson

e. Henry

f. Katherine

✪ Read the sentences. Circle Yes or No.

1. Katherine's apartment manager is her friend. (YES) NO
2. The manager wants Rosa to rent the apartment. YES NO
3. The manager rents the apartment to Rosa. YES NO
4. Katherine decides the manager is not her friend. YES NO

✪✪ Put the sentences in order. Number 1 to 5.

_____ The manager tells Rosa the apartment is rented.

__1__ Rosa wants to move.

_____ The Crossroads Café workers decide to prove that Dorothy Walsh discriminated against Rosa.

_____ There is an apartment for rent in Katherine's building.

_____ Katherine discovers the apartment is not rented.

✪✪✪ Write the story. Use the five sentences above. Add these three sentences. Then close the book and tell the story to someone.

- Rosa decides to file a complaint.
- The apartment manager offers the apartment to Patty Peterson and her father.
- Rosa can't sleep because of noisy heat and water pipes in her apartment building.

Rosa can't sleep because of noisy heat and water pipes in her apartment building. Rosa

wants to move.

_____

_____

_____

_____

_____

_____

_____

_____

_____

Your New Language: Asking for Clarification

It's a fantastic apartment, lots of room, and the pipes don't talk to themselves.

The pipes? I don't understand.

The plumbing, Mr. Brashov.

To clarify something you don't understand, you can ask:

- **What does that mean?**
- **What do you mean?**

You can also

- say, "I don't understand."
- repeat the words you don't understand: "The pipes don't talk."
  "What do you mean, the pipes don't talk?"
- ask a question: "You mean the plumbing is quiet?"

⭐ Complete the conversations. Use these words and phrases.

a little mix up   not settled   not our type   significant

1.

There's been a little mix up.

What do you mean, **a little mix up** ?

2.

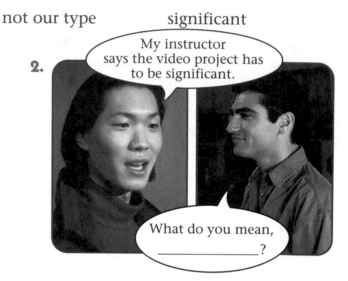

My instructor says the video project has to be significant.

What do you mean, _____?

3.

Not everything is settled.

What do you mean, _____?

4.

She's not our type.

What do you mean, _____?

✪✪ Match.

1. Your kind isn't wanted here.
2. This camera has been designed with simplicity in mind.
3. Discrimination comes in a lot of different packages.
4. Henry's journalism class is going to work with video cameras.
5. It's next to the manual focus control.

a. What do you mean?
b. You mean they do more than write stories?
c. You mean because I speak with an accent?
d. You mean this button?
e. What does simplicity mean?

✪✪✪ Complete the conversation. Use these phrases. You may use a phrase more than once. Write one in each blank. (Sometimes there is more than one correct answer.)

| I mean | do you mean | What do you mean? |
| that means | you mean | What does that mean? |

KATHERINE: When does she move in to the apartment?

DOROTHY: I don't know. She hasn't decided if she's going to take it.

KATHERINE: ___Do you mean___ the apartment's not rented?
(1)

DOROTHY: No, not yet. But keep your fingers crossed.

KATHERINE: I'm confused. You told Rosa it was rented.

DOROTHY: Rosa? Oh, _____ that little Mexican girl. Not quite
(2)

our type.

KATHERINE: Not our type? _____
(3)

DOROTHY: _____ she's different from us. The other tenants
(4)

wouldn't be comfortable with her.

KATHERINE: Dorothy Walsh. _____ that you won't rent to someone
(5)

from another country? That's discrimination!

✪ Put the conversation in order. Number 1 to 3.

____ JAMAL: Try the button next to the focus control.

____ HENRY: You mean this one?

_1_ HENRY: Where's the on/off button?

✪✪ Put the conversation in order. Number 1 to 5.

____ JAMAL: Discriminate? What exactly does that mean?

____ KATHERINE: Dorothy Walsh is a sweet woman. She would never discriminate against anyone.

____ JAMAL: You mean, like charge one person more than another for the same thing?

____ JESS: It means to treat different people differently.

____ JESS: That's right. Or tell someone an apartment is already rented because you don't like the color of his or her skin.

✪✪✪ Put the conversation in order. Number 1 to 6.

____ JESS: A little mix up? That's a bad sign.

____ MR. BRASHOV: Rosa didn't get the apartment. The manager told her there was a little mix up.

____ JESS: I mean I've heard "there's been a little mix up" a lot in my life. It means someone doesn't want her.

____ MR. BRASHOV: What do you mean, a bad sign?

____ MR. BRASHOV: You mean Katherine's apartment manager is discriminating against Rosa?

____ MR. BRASHOV: I'm afraid so.

In Your Community: Rental Applications

This is the rental application that Rosa filled out for the apartment. Answer the questions about the information on the form. Then share your answers with someone.

RENTAL APPLICATION

I __Rosa Rivera__ hereby apply to rent Apartment __#210__ at __34 Lincoln Ave.__ Proposed occupants:
spouse or co-resident __N/A__ Children: # __0__ Names: __N/A__

Applicant Information

Please submit the following information. Move-in monies must be paid in cashier checks, money orders, or travelers checks.
Applicant __Rosa Rivera__ Soc. Sec. # __540-46-7951__ Birth Date __7/21/70__ Valid Dr. Lic. # __N/A__
State __N/A__ Address __493 Main St. Apt. C__ City/State __Middletown, IL__ How long __2 yrs.__ Rent
per month __$600.00__ Telephone No. __555-8831__ Landlord __Cesar Melendez__ Telephone No. __555-2748__

EMPLOYMENT AND CREDIT INFORMATION

Employment
Employed by __Crossroads Café__ How long __6 months__ Position __cook__ Salary __$1300.00/month__
Address __2950 West 53rd St.__ City/State __Middletown, IL__ Phone # __555-2345__

Bank Information
Bank __National Bank__ Branch/City/State __0379 Middletown, IL__
Checking Account # __486-32-7724__ Savings Account # _____

Major Credit Cards
Name __Uni Bank__ # __4734 8910 5467__ Outstanding Balance __$0.00__
Name __N/A__ # _____ Outstanding Balance __$_____

REFERENCES

Relative or Friend __Katherine Blake__ Relationship __work together__ Address __34 Lincoln Ave. Apt. 108__
City/State __Middletown, IL__ Tel # __555-4206__ How long known __6 months__

Everything that I have stated in this application is correct to the best of my knowledge. I authorize you to obtain and provide information for the purpose of verification of any part of this rental application.
Date: __Sept. 5, 1996__ Applicant: __Rosa Rivera__

★ 1. How long has Rosa lived at her current address? _____

2. How much rent does she pay now? _____

★★ 1. Whose name does Rosa give as a reference? _____

2. Does Rosa drive? How do you know? _____

★★★ 1. Does Rosa plan to share her new apartment with someone? How do you know?

_____

2. Does Rosa owe any money on her credit cards? How do you know?

_____

Now get a rental application from an apartment building, other housing, or check the forms section of a stationery store in your community. How is it the same as or different from the one above?

Read and Write: Spotlight on Katherine

Read the questions. Read Katherine's diary entry very quickly to find the answers. Circle the answers.

★ What does Katherine write about?
   a. the people at the café
   b. her apartment manager
   c. Rosa's apartment

★★ How does Katherine feel about Dorothy?
   a. Katherine thinks Dorothy is sweet.
   b. Katherine is mad at Dorothy.
   c. Katherine doesn't want Dorothy as a friend.

★★★ What is the tone, or feeling, of this letter?
   a. disappointed
   b. happy
   c. angry

Read the diary entry again carefully.

Find the words in the reading that mean the same as the phrases below. Write the words below the phrases.

★ treating someone differently

_____

★★ to tell a tenant to move out

_____

★★★ a person who can make statements about another person's character

_____

Saturday, 11:30 P.M.
Day, Time

My Diary. . .

Dorothy Walsh, my apartment building manager, was my friend. But not after what she did to Rosa.

Rosa tried to rent an apartment in my building. Dorothy told Rosa it was already rented. Jess thought Dorothy was discriminating against Rosa. Rosa speaks English with an accent and has a Mexican name. I didn't think Dorothy would treat her differently from other people. Then I found Dorothy showing the apartment Rosa had looked at. It wasn't rented! Rosa gave my name as a reference, but Dorothy never asked me about Rosa.

My friends at the café decided to prove that Dorothy discriminated against Rosa. Jess, Jamal, and Mr. Brashov all looked at the apartment. She actually told them, "Your kind is not welcome here." Henry got it all on videotape. Rosa is going to file a complaint.

Dorothy is mad at me, too. She may try to evict me. She had better not tell me to move out. I will take her to court. I want to keep my apartment, but I don't want to keep a friend like Dorothy!

Now you write a diary entry about an act of discrimination against you or someone you know. In your entry answer the following questions.

✪ Where did it happen?
Who discriminated?
Who was discriminated against?
Why do you think someone discriminated against the person?

✪✪ When did it happen?
How was the person treated differently?
What did the person who was discriminated against do about it?

✪✪✪ What would you do if this happened to you?

Day, Time

My Diary...

Day, Time

My Diary...

Read your entry to someone. Then ask: Did you understand? Do you have questions?

What Do You Think?

✪ Rosa likes the apartment. At first, Dorothy will not rent the apartment to Rosa. Then she offers Rosa the apartment. What do you think Rosa should do?

1. She should take the apartment.   YES   NO   I DON'T KNOW

2. She should report Dorothy to the Fair Housing Bureau. YES   NO   I DON'T KNOW

✪✪ Look at the sentences below. Check (✓) I agree, I disagree, or I don't know.

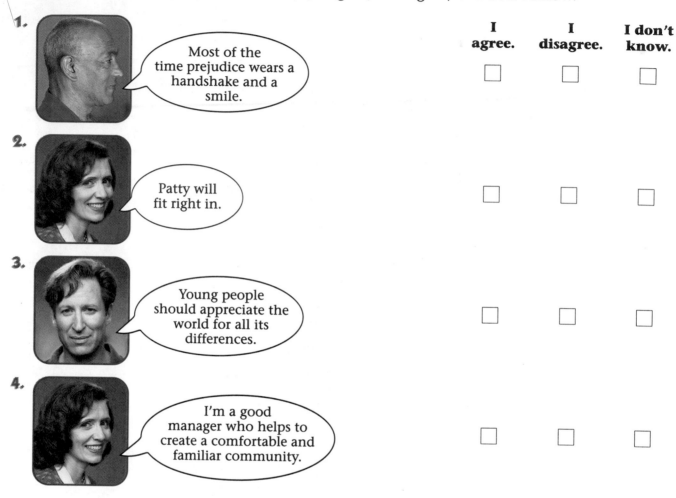

	I agree.	I disagree.	I don't know.
1. Most of the time prejudice wears a handshake and a smile.	☐	☐	☐
2. Patty will fit right in.	☐	☐	☐
3. Young people should appreciate the world for all its differences.	☐	☐	☐
4. I'm a good manager who helps to create a comfortable and familiar community.	☐	☐	☐

✪✪✪ Answer the questions. Then read your answers to someone.

1. Do you think that prejudice wears a handshake and a smile?
   Tell why or why not.

_____

2. Would you want your children to appreciate the world for all its differences?
   Tell why or why not.

_____

3. Do you fit right in in this country? Tell why or why not.

_____

4. Do you think that Dorothy is a good manager? Tell why or why not.

_____

Culture Clip: Discrimination

✪ Match.

1. Sometimes people judge others because of race, color, or gender.

   a.

2. Sometimes people don't listen.

   b.

3. Some people want others to be like them.

   c.

✪✪ Complete the sentences. Write one word in each blank. Use these words.

different	laws	reason	fear
opinion	result	group	prejudice
woman			

Incidents of prejudice have occurred throughout history. __Prejudice__ is hostility of one
                                                                (1)
_____ toward another group. It is judging, or forming an _____, that is not based on
   (2)   (3)
logic, _____, or fact. Some people think a _____ who is a wife and mother can't do a
          (4)   (5)
job. Some people think a person who is a _____ color can't do a job. Prejudice may be the
                                             (6)
result of ignorance about, or _____ of, people who aren't just like them. It may also be the
                                  (7)
_____ of economic pressure. The United States Congress has passed _____ in response
   (8)   (9)
to discrimination in housing and in the workplace.

✪✪✪ Dorothy Walsh told Rosa there was some sort of mix up, and that the apartment had already been rented. Do you think Dorothy Walsh was prejudiced? Write your ideas. Then tell your ideas to someone.

_____

_____

_____

Check Your English

⭐ Write the correct word or phrase under each picture.

an excited
   person

tape measure

videotape

video camera

a big smile

a person
   pointing

1.
an excited person

2.
_____

3.
_____

4.
_____

5.
_____

6.
_____

⭐⭐ Make a sentence or question from each group of words.

1. you   button   this   mean   do

   Do you mean this button?
_____

2. does   what   mean   discrimination

_____

_____

3. information   without   means   prejudice   deciding

_____

_____

4. treat   discriminate   differently   to   means   people

_____

_____

⭐⭐⭐ Finish the story. Use the words in the box. Write one word or phrase in each blank.

Rosa looks at an apartment in Katherine's __building__ . She fills out a rental
                                                                     (1)

_____ and gives it to Dorothy Walsh, the building _____ . A few
  (2)   (3)

days later, Dorothy tells Rosa that the apartment is already rented. Then

Dorothy shows the _____ to a young lady and her father. Katherine
                    (4)

realizes the apartment is not _____ . Rosa's friends at Crossroads Café
                             (5)

decide to prove _____ against Rosa. Mr. Brashov, Jamal, and Jess try
               (6)

to _____ the apartment. Henry hides in a corner with his _____ .
  (7)   (8)

The father decides he won't sign the rental _____ . Threatened by the
                                         (9)

_____ , Dorothy offers the apartment to Rosa. Rosa turns it down and
  (10)

decides to file a complaint.

apartment
application
building
discrimination
lease
manager
rent
rental
rented
right
video camera
videotape
wrong

12 Turning Points

In this unit you will:

- express possibilities
- read a police crime log
- write a newspaper article
- identify solutions to gang problems

Ways to Learn

There's a problem at the café. The workers and community members *act* to solve the problem. *Being active* in your community can help you learn English.

Be Active

Check (✓) ways you are *active* in your community.

- ☐ I visit a neighbor.
- ☐ I volunteer at a school.
- ☐ I volunteer at a hospital.
- ☐ I am a member of a group.
- ☐ I visit a community center.
- ☐ I attend neighborhood meetings.
- ☐ I visit my child's teacher.
- ☐ other:

On Your Own

Last month I *was active* in my community by

_____

I learned about

_____

Next month, I plan to

_____

Before You Watch

Look at the pictures. What do you see?

1.

2.

3.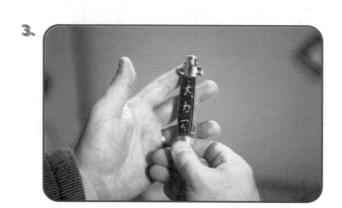

4.

5.

6.

✪ What do you see in each picture? Write the number of the picture next to the word.

  5   bruise   ____ spray paint

____ knife   ____ gang

____ graffiti   ____ crime report

✪✪ What is happening? Write the number of the picture next to the sentence.

  3   Mr. Brashov finds a knife.

____ A boy is holding a can of spray paint.

____ The floor is covered with broken glasses and dishes and graffiti is on the walls.

____ A boy has several bruises.

____ The police officer is writing a crime report.

____ Gang members are standing in the café.

✪✪✪ Write one question you have about each picture. Then read your questions to someone.

1. What happened at Crossroads Café? _____

2. _____

3. _____

4. _____

5. _____

6. _____

Focus For Watching   Read the questions. Then watch.

✪ 1. Who is the leader of The Dragons?
   2. Who is a member of The Dragons?

✪✪ 1. Whose knife is found?
    2. Who suggests calling the police?

✪✪✪ 1. Who teaches Edward to defend himself?
     2. Who suggests a plan to stop the gang?

After You Watch

What do you remember? Match each question with the correct picture. You can use a picture more than once.

⭐ 1. Who is the leader of The Dragons?

a. Henry

2. Who is a member of The Dragons?

b. Mr. Brashov

⭐⭐ 1. Whose knife is found?

c. Johnny

2. Who suggests calling the police?

d. Edward

⭐⭐⭐ 1. Who teaches Edward to defend himself?

e. Rosa

2. Who suggests a plan to stop the gang?

✪ Read the sentences. Circle Yes or No.
1. Edward is in a gang.   (YES)   NO
2. The gang takes money from the café.   YES   NO
3. The knife is Henry's.   YES   NO
4. Edward tells Henry about the gang.   YES   NO
5. Edward helps the police catch the gang.   YES   NO

✪✪ Put the sentences in order. Number 1 to 5.

_____ Henry recognizes the knife.

_____ The police surround the gang members, handcuff them, and take them away.

__1__ Mr. Brashov arrives one morning and finds that the café has been vandalized.

_____ Mr. Brashov sees a knife with Chinese lettering in the wall.

_____ Edward tells Henry about the gang.

✪✪✪ Write the story. Use the five sentences above. Add these three sentences.
Then close the book and tell the story to someone.
- Edward brings the gang to the café to help the police catch the gang.
- Mr. Brashov has a plan to catch the gang.
- There is graffiti spray painted on the walls.

  Mr. Brashov arrives one morning and finds that the café has been vandalized.

_____

_____

_____

_____

_____

_____

_____

_____

_____

_____

_____

Your New Language: Expressing Possibilities

To talk about something that you are not sure is true, you can say:

- Someone **might** still **be** in there.
- There **might be** fingerprints.

⭐ Complete the conversations. Use these phrases.

someday you   beat me up   upset   in there

1.

2.

3.

4.

✪✪ Match.

1. And who do you have here?
2. Someone might still be in there.
3. Anyone in the neighborhood who might be upset?
4. Look at this knife!
5. Do you think this will make a difference?

a. It might. It might not.
b. No. Why would anyone be angry?
c. You're right. You stay here.
d. It might belong to Henry.
e. This might be one of the kids who broke in the other night.

✪✪✪ Complete the conversation. Use these words or phrases. Write one in each blank. You may use a word or phrase more than once.

might not have   might think   might help   might bite   might

POLICE: This neighborhood has had some problems recently. You should think of some additional security measures.

ROSA: Do you think leaving lights on at night ___might help___ ?
(1)

POLICE: It _____ .
(2)

JAMAL: There are lots of things we could do. We could put bars on the windows.

KATHERINE: Yeah, but people _____ this was a jail!
(3)

JAMAL: Maybe we could get a security dog.

ROSA: Right, and the dog _____ our customers.
(4)

MR. BRASHOV: If we don't get to work, we _____ any more customers!
(5)

✪ Put the conversation in order. Number 1 to 3.

<u> 1 </u> JAMAL: Do you think the gang will come back?

_____ JAMAL: Well, we'll be ready for them.

_____ MR. BRASHOV: They might come.

✪✪ Put the conversation in order. Number 1 to 4.

_____ ROSA: It's the gang's way of telling us that they are strong.

_____ ROSA: Look at this knife with Chinese lettering. Who does it belong to?

_____ KATHERINE: Why do you think it was in the wall?

_____ MR. BRASHOV: It might belong to Henry. He might have left it here when he was opening boxes.

✪✪✪ Put the conversation in order. Number 1 to 6.

_____ JAMAL: I'd better wait then. I'll check the storeroom for paint. I might need to buy some to cover up the graffiti.

_____ MR. BRASHOV: Yes. Actually, we might be closed for a few days.

_____ MR. BRASHOV: Be careful not to touch anything. There might be fingerprints.

_____ JAMAL: Oh. Well, I'll start to clean up.

_____ MR. BRASHOV: Check to see if we have trash bags. You might need to buy some of those, too.

_____ JAMAL: Do you want me to make a sign that we will be closed today?

In Your Community: Police Crime Log

This is a summary of all the crimes reported last week. It appears in the local newspaper every week.

Police Crime Log

The following crimes were reported to the Police Department. Residents are listed by street name only. Times listed indicate when incidents were reported.

Petty Theft—3:57 P.M. Walnut Avenue - Juveniles took potted plants.

Theft—10:30 A.M. Fairfield Blvd. - Woman's bicycle taken.

Auto Burglary—10:30 P.M. Katella Avenue - Suspect smashed window, suspect took phone and briefcase.

Fight—10:40 P.M. Marine Avenue - Two males, and a female.

Vandalism—5:00 P.M. West 53rd St. - gang-related, graffiti on walls, broken dishes, overturned furniture, entry through front door, suspects still at large, no evidence of theft.

Auto Theft—3:41 P.M. Baton Road - 1984 Mitsubishi Mirage taken.

Read the Police Crime Log. Circle Yes or No.

✪ 1. Someone took a woman's bicycle. (YES)   NO

2. Someone took an automobile. YES   NO

✪✪ 1. Several things were stolen from Crossroads Café. YES   NO

2. The petty theft was committed by adults. YES   NO

✪✪✪ 1. The auto theft happened at 3:41 P.M. YES   NO

2. According to this log, the Crossroads Café suspects were captured. YES   NO

Look at a crime log in your local newspaper. How is it the same as or different from the one above?

Read and Write: Spotlight on Henry

Henry wrote this article for the school newspaper.
Read the questions. Read Henry's article very
quickly to find the answers. Circle the answers.

✪ 1. What did Henry write about?
   a. his brother   b. a crime   c. money

✪✪ 1. How does he feel?
   a. upset   b. discouraged   c. pleased

✪✪✪ 1. What is the tone or feeling of the article?
   a. humorous   b. serious   c. alarming

Read the newspaper article again carefully.

> **CRIME DOESN'T PAY**
> by Henry Chang
>
> Last week, the café I work at was vandalized. My boss arrived at the café in the morning. The door was open and the window was shattered. The floor was covered with broken glass and dishes. The furniture was overturned. There was graffiti on the walls. We were angry. Everything was a mess! The owner called the police. When the police came, they told us a local gang had wrecked the café. What the gang did was wrong. The employees, neighbors, and business owners joined together and helped the police catch the gang members. Crime doesn't pay and it didn't pay for The Dragons. We're not sure if we made a difference, but it's a beginning.

Which words or phrases in the note are similar to the words or phrases below?
Write your answers in the blanks.

✪ 1. chairs and tables _____

   2. employer _____

✪✪ 1. upside-down _____

   2. not right _____

✪✪✪ 1. to have destroyed property _____

   2. broken into little pieces _____

Write a newspaper article about a crime. In your article answer the following questions.

✪ 1. When did it happen?
   2. Who was vandalized?
   3. Where did it happen?

✪✪ 1. How did it happen?
    2. What did the person who was vandalized do?

✪✪✪ 1. What would you do if it happened to you?

by ⸻

Read your article to someone. Then ask: Did you understand? Do you have questions?

What Do You Think?

✪ Edward has a problem with a gang. Who should he tell? Check (✓).

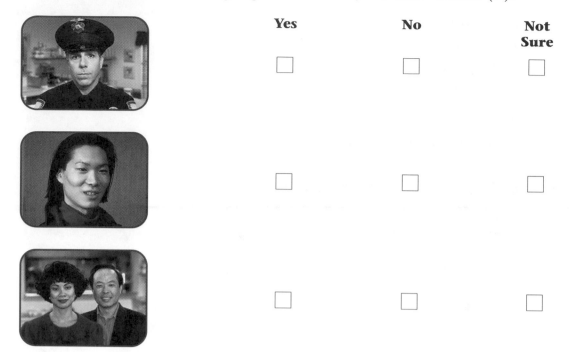

	Yes	No	Not Sure
	☐	☐	☐
	☐	☐	☐
	☐	☐	☐

✪✪ Look at the sentences below. Check (✓) I agree, I disagree, or I don't know.

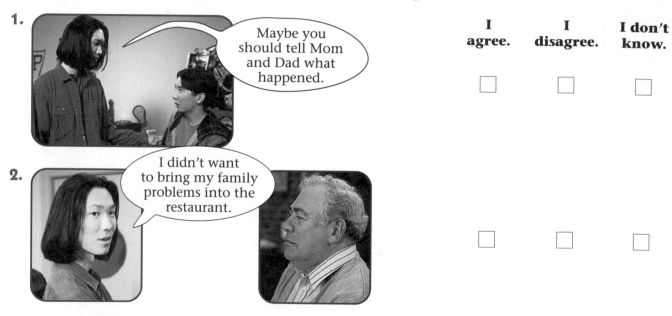

1. Maybe you should tell Mom and Dad what happened.

	I agree.	I disagree.	I don't know.
1.	☐	☐	☐
2.	☐	☐	☐

2. I didn't want to bring my family problems into the restaurant.

✪✪✪ Answer the questions. Then read your answers to someone.

1. Do you think children should always tell their parents about their problems? Tell why or why not.

_____

2. Do you think employees should talk about their personal problems at work? Tell why or why not.

_____

Culture Clip: Solutions to Gang Problems

✪ Match.

1. Teachers can be models for their students.

2. Role-plays in classes help students learn to say no.

3. Students need support from people they can identify with.

4. Adults recognize students for the good things they do.

a.

b.

c.

d.

✪✪ Complete the sentences. Use these words.

gangs	country	teach	community
dangers	choices	skills	programs
differences			

Across the __country__ , schools and _____ groups are uniting to _____ children the
         (1)   (2)   (3)

dangers of joining _____ . In classrooms students are being taught the _____ they need
                        (4)   (5)

to say no to gangs. They are taught to make good _____ . Adults who were once involved
                                                        (6)

with gangs are often part of _____ that help students see the _____ of gangs. These
                                  (7)   (8)

programs make _____ in the lives of the students and their families.
                   (9)

✪✪✪ Henry and his friends at Crossroads Café join to fight the neighborhood gang. Do you
think it's important to stop gangs in your community? Tell why or why not? If yes,
what are some ways to do this? Write your ideas. Then tell your ideas to someone.

_____

_____

_____

Check Your English

✪ Write the correct word under each picture.

graffiti

gang

crime report

knife

spray paint

bruise

1. _____

2. _____

3. _____

4. _____

5. _____

6. graffiti

✪✪ Make a sentence or question from each group of words.

1. gang   think   the   might   do   come   you   back

   Do you think the gang might come back?

2. this   make   difference   a   might

   _____

3. café   we   have   close   for   might   the   several   to   days

   _____

4. with   there   upset   anyone   who   is   might   be   you

   _____

✪✪✪ Finish the story. Use the words in the box. Write one word in each blank.

Early one morning Mr. Brashov arrives at Crossroads Café. He finds the

____door____ open, the furniture overturned, and _____ on the wall.
    (1)   (2)

The police come and take a _____. A _____ has _____ the
                              (3)   (4)   (5)

café. Mr. Brashov notices a knife on the wall. Henry recognizes the

_____. It belongs to his brother. Edward tells Henry that the gang has
   (6)

forced him to _____. He has _____ on his back. Henry is angry
               (7)   (8)

with his brother, but says nothing. Mr. Brashov has a plan to _____
                                                                  (9)

the gang. Edward helps Mr. Brashov. One night he brings the gang to

Crossroads Café. The police _____ the gang and take them away. The
                              (10)

employees are not sure if they made a difference, but it's a good beginning.

bruises
catch
crime report
door
fight
gang
graffiti
join
knife
money
surround
vandalized

13 Trading Places

In this unit you will:

- tell someone about the things you can do
- read and understand a help wanted ad
- write a note of apology
- describe the roles couples choose

Ways to Learn

At Crossroads Café, the employees try to *observe* and learn from each other so they can work better together. They *watch* and learn. One way to learn English is to *observe others*.

Observe Others

Circle who or what you *watch* or *observe* to learn English.

Who do you *watch at home* to learn English?
a. a neighbor
b. family members
c. does not apply

Who do you *watch at work* to learn English?
a. my supervisor
b. a coworker
c. does not apply

Who do you *watch at school* to learn English?
a. my teacher
b. a classmate
c. does not apply

What do you *watch on T.V.* to learn English?
a. news
b. educational programs
c. stories

On Your Own

List the people you *watched* last week. What did you *observe?*

Who	What
_____	_____
_____	_____
_____	_____

Before You Watch

Look at the pictures. What do you see?

1.

2.

3.

4.

5.

6.

✪ What do you see in each picture? Write the number of the picture next to the word.

_1_ waiter   ____ cook

____ handyman   ____ delivery person

____ manager   ____ busboy

✪✪ What is happening? Write the number of the picture next to the sentence.

____ Rosa is taking money from a customer at the cash register.

____ Jamal is delivering the take-out orders.

_1_ Henry is waiting on tables.

____ Mr. Brashov is fixing something.

____ Katherine is cooking lunch in the kitchen.

____ Jamal is pushing a cart.

✪✪✪ Write one question you have about each picture. Then read your questions to someone.

1. _Why is Henry waiting on tables?_____

2. _____

3. _____

4. _____

5. _____

6. _____

Focus For Watching   Read the questions. Then watch.

✪ 1. Who is cooking?
2. Who is delivering the food?
3. Who is giving the customers change?
4. Who is serving the food?

✪✪ 1. Who says the customer is the most important person in the café?
2. Who decides that the employees will trade jobs for one day?

✪✪✪ 1. Who thinks that the café will lose some business because of the experiment?
2. Who says that Mr. Brashov thinks he is the only one that can manage the café?

After You Watch

What do you remember? Match each question with the correct picture. You can use a picture more than once.

In Today's Show . . .

⭐ 1. Who is cooking?

2. Who is delivering the food?

3. Who is giving the customers change?

4. Who is serving the food?

⭐⭐ 1. Who says the customer is the most important person in the café?

2. Who decides that the employees will trade jobs for one day?

⭐⭐⭐ 1. Who thinks that the café will lose some business because of the experiment?

2. Who says that Mr. Brashov thinks he is the only one that can manage the café?

a. Mr. Brashov

b. Rosa

c. Henry

d. Katherine

e. Jamal

f. Jess

✪ Read the sentences and check (✓) Yes or No. If the answer is No, write the correct job.

In Today's Show . . .	Yes	No	Correct Job
1. Katherine is the customer.		✓	cook
2. Rosa is the boss/manager.			
3. Mr. Brashov is the handyman.			
4. Jess is the customer.			
5. Henry is the handyman.			
6. Jamal is the delivery man and busboy.			

✪✪ Put the sentences in order. Number 1 to 5.

_____ Everyone has a new job. Katherine is cooking; Rosa is giving the customers change; Jamal is delivering take-out orders; and Henry is serving food.

_____ Mr. Brashov plans an experiment to have his employees change jobs for a day.

__1__ The employees at Crossroads Café are arguing about whose job is the most important.

_____ It's lunchtime and the regular customers arrive for their meals. There are too many customers.

_____ Customers are yelling for their food and waiting for their change. Take-out orders are late. The experiment is not working.

✪✪✪ Write the story. Use the five sentences above. Add these three sentences. Then close the book and tell the story to someone.
- Each employee thinks his or her job is the most important.
- Everyone thinks that the new jobs they are doing are very easy.
- The customers are very unhappy.

The employees at Crossroads Café are arguing about whose job is the most important.

_____

_____

_____

_____

_____

_____

Your New Language: Talking about Ability

Rosa, you're not the only one who knows how to cook. I'm a mother. I can cook.

And I fix things around my apartment all the time. That doesn't mean I can do Jamal's job.

To express ability or inability to do something, you can say:

- I **can** cook.
- I **can't** cook.
- I **know how to** cook.
- I **don't know how to** cook.

⭐ Complete the conversations. Use these words.

manage	afford	repair	make

1.

What can you cook?

I can <u>make</u> tuna sandwiches and spaghetti.

2.

Who will fix things around here?

I'll give it a try. I can _____ things around here.

3.

We only eat out on Saturday. We can't afford to eat out more than once a week.

We can _____ a few extras, like going out to dinner.

4.

How can I possibly take a vacation?

He doesn't think we can _____ the café.

✪✪ Match.

1. The stove isn't working.
2. Do you know how to speak Spanish?
3. I know how to learn English quickly.
4. She doesn't know how to play tennis.
5. Do you know how to cook?

a. No, I don't, but I'm studying.
b. Yes, I do. Italian cooking is my speciality.
c. Let's teach her.
d. So do I. Watch Crossroads Café.
e. I know how to fix that. It's electric, isn't it?

What do you know how to do? _____

_____

_____

_____

✪✪✪ Complete the conversation. Use these words and phrases. Write one in each blank. You may use a word or phrase more than once.

can   can't   know how to   don't know how to

JESS: We _____can't_____ afford to eat out more than one night a week.
                        (1)

CAROL: Yes, we can, Jess. There are some things that we _____ afford
             to do now that I'm working.   (2)

JESS: And, I'm telling you that we _____. Look at these bills.
                                          (3)

CAROL: I saw those bills. I paid some of them last night.

JESS: You _____ do that!
                        (4)

CAROL: Yes, I do, Jess. I _____ add and subtract just like you.
                              (5)

✪ Put the conversation in order. Number 1 to 4.

____	KATHERINE:	No, I can't, but I can learn.
____	KATHERINE:	Sure. I can make spaghetti with meat sauce.
____	ROSA:	Well, can you cook Mexican food?
__1__	ROSA:	Can you cook Italian food?

✪✪ Put the conversation in order. Number 1 to 4.

____	JAMAL:	Thanks. I'll let you know.
____	JAMAL:	Yes, but I may need some help. I can't do it by myself.
____	MR. BRASHOV:	I can help. Let me know when I can help you.
____	MR. BRASHOV:	There's a leak in the water pipe in the utility room. Do you know how to repair it?

✪✪✪ Put the conversation in order. Number 1 to 5.

____	MR. BRASHOV:	I don't know. But, Katherine can do that.
____	JESS:	I don't know. Does she know how to work the cash register?
____	MR. BRASHOV:	I think so. But if she doesn't know how to do that, I can teach her.
____	JESS:	Can she place the order for the supplies?
____	MR. BRASHOV:	Do you think Rosa can manage the café?

In Your Community: Help Wanted Ads

✪ Read the help wanted ad for Katherine's job. Check (✓) Yes or No.

		Yes	No
Food Server **Waitress or Waiter** Friendly, fast, helpful person with family restaurant experience needed. Full-time (FT) day position M-F. Call Crossroads Café for appt. (217) 555-2345 Ask for Mr. Brashov.	1. You need to go to the restaurant and talk to Mr. Brashov about the job.	✓	
	2. A food server is a waiter or waitress.		
	3. The job is at night.		
	4. Experience is necessary.		
	5. The job is 25 hours per week.		

✪✪ Read the help wanted ad for Henry's job. Check (✓) Yes, No, or Don't Know.
If you check Don't Know, write questions you would ask to get the information.

		Yes	No	Don't Know
	1. This job pays minimum wage.			✓
Bus/Delivery Person Part time, energetic, dependable, flexible person w/own transportation to work in restaurant. Will train. Call btw 2-4 PM (217) 555-2345.	2. The job pays mileage.			
	3. The hours for this job are between 2–4 P.M.			
	4. Experience is required.			
	5. This person can work 10–15 hours per week.			
	6. This person must have a car or bicycle.			

Your Questions: _____

_____

✪✪✪ Read the following help wanted ad for Jamal's job. Check (✓) Yes or No. If Yes,
circle and number the information in the ad that supports your answer.

		Yes	No
Handyman #1 Looking for honest, dependable quality-minded individual to take care of restaurant repair needs. Exp in carpentry, plumbing, electrical. Some painting needed. Apply in person. Crossroads Café. 2950 W. 53rd St.	1. This person must come to work regularly.	✓	
	2. The individual must know how to build tables, fix leaky faucets, and repair wires.		
	3. The repair work must be done well.		
	4. Only men should apply.		

Find a help wanted ad in the classified section of your newspaper. How is your help
wanted ad the same as or different from the help wanted ads above?

Read and Write: Spotlight on Jess

Read the questions. Read Jess's note to his wife very quickly to find the answers. Circle the answers.

✪ What does Jess write about?
   a. a gift for his wife
   b. a gift from his wife

✪✪ How does Jess feel about his marriage?
   a. angry
   b. lucky
   c. sad

✪✪✪ What is the tone or feeling of this letter?
   a. apologetic   b. angry   c. cheerful

Read the note again carefully.

> Dear Carol,
>
> I'm sorry about the watch. It's a great gift and I really like it. I am very lucky to have someone as special as you. I want you to know that I am going to stop feeling sorry for myself and start enjoying life a little more. So, how about going to that new restaurant tonight, even though it's not Saturday?
>
>   Love, Jess
>
> P.S. You pay. You can afford it!

Find the words in the reading. What do they mean? Circle the answer.

✪ Gift:
   a. a watch   b. a sweater   c. both of these

✪✪ to afford something:
   a. to have enough   b. to throw it away   c. to sell it
     money to buy it

✪✪✪ to feel sorry for oneself:
   a. to be sad   b. to smile   c. to laugh

Now you write a note to someone. Tell about something you did that you are sorry about. In your note answer the following questions.

⭐ 1. What did you do?

2. How do you feel?

⭐⭐ Why did you do it?

⭐⭐⭐ What you are going to do to make things better?

Read your note to someone. Then ask: Did you understand? Do you have questions?

What Do You Think?

⭐ Which person do you think has the most important job at Crossroads Café?
Circle the picture of the person. Why do you think so?

⭐⭐ Look at the sentences below. Check (✓) I agree, I disagree, or I don't know.

	I agree.	I disagree.	I don't know.
1. Anyone could manage the café without me. Everyone here is of equal importance.	☐	☐	☐
2. Without my cooking, the café would not do so well.	☐	☐	☐
3. The customer is the most important person.	☐	☐	☐
4. This cooking job isn't so tough.	☐	☐	☐
5. Being a waiter is not such a difficult job.	☐	☐	☐

⭐⭐⭐ Answer the questions. Then read your answers to someone.

1. Do you think that everyone at Crossroads Café is important? Tell why or why not.

_____

2. Do you think that the customer is the most important person? Tell why or why not.

_____

Culture Clip: The Roles Couples Choose

✪ Match.

1. Peter Chu is the cook in the family.

a.

2. Irene Cruz is ironing.

b.

3. Mrs. Estelle is teaching.

c.

✪✪ Complete the sentences. Write one word in each blank. Use these words.

responsibilities	roles	rules	couple
determine	wrong	marriage	right
patterns			

Husbands and wives play many different ___roles___ during their
                    (1)

_____. Some follow the _____ of their parents. Some don't.
 (2)   (3)

There are no _____. Each _____ must _____ their own rules.
         (4)   (5)   (6)

There is no _____ or _____ way for couples to share _____.
        (7)   (8)   (9)

✪✪✪ Think.

"There is no right or wrong way for couples to share family responsibilities. They must choose roles that work for them."

Do you agree with this statement? Why or why not? Write your ideas. Then tell your ideas to someone.

_____

_____

_____

_____

Check Your English

✪ Write the correct word under each picture.

waiter

cook

handyman

delivery person

busboy

manager

1.

waiter

2.

3.

4.

5.

6.

✪✪ Make a sentence or question from each group of words.

1. a   cook   Rosa   meal   can   delicious

Rosa can cook a delicious meal. OR _Can Rosa cook a delicious meal?_

2. quickly   can   Katherine   take   orders

_____

3. speak   Rosa   how   Spanish   to   knows

_____

4. know   you   how   English   to   speak   do

_____

✪✪✪ Finish the story. Use the words in the box. Write one word in each blank.

The employees at Crossroads Café are arguing about whose ___job___ (1)

is the most _____. To show his employees that all jobs are equally (2)

important, Mr. Brashov tries an _____. He has his employees (3)

_____ jobs for a day. For a little while the experiment works. Katherine (4)

is _____. Rosa is bossing _____ around. Jamal is _____ (5) (6) (7)

take-out orders and Henry is _____ food. However, when the (8)

_____ crowd arrives, things change quickly. _____ are yelling (9) (10)

for their food and waiting impatiently for their change. The experiment

is not working.

change
cooking
customers
delivering
dinner
equal
experiment
important
job
lunchtime
people
serving

Teacher/Tutor Appendix

If you have read the section *To the Learner* at the beginning of this book, the information in this appendix will provide a more detailed understanding of the scope and the goals of the program. The *Crossroads Café* print and video materials are closely correlated to provide everything needed for successful, non-stressful language-learning experiences, either alone or with a teacher or tutor.

The *Worktexts*

The two *Crossroads Café Worktexts* provide multi-level language activities with three levels of challenge: Beginning High, Intermediate Low and Intermediate High (or SPL 4, 5, and 6). These activities are visually designated in the *Worktext* as ✪, ✪✪, or ✪✪✪, respectively. The 1-star exercises ask learners to communicate using words and phrases; responses are frequently based on a visual stimulus. The 2-star exercises ask learners to communicate using learned phrases and structures; responses may be based on visual stimulus or text. The 3-star exercises are designed for students who can participate in basic conversation; responses are most often based on text not visuals. *Worktext* unit exercises develop *story comprehension, language skills,* and *higher order thinking* and they provide practice in reading, writing, and speaking. Every *Worktext* unit opens with a photo depicting the theme of the storyline, a list of learning objectives, and a learning strategy.

Crossroads Café Worktext Framework

	Exercise Section	Purpose	✪	✪✪	✪✪✪
Story Comprehension (Video)	*Before You Watch*	Preview storyline vocabulary and events.	Match words with video photos to highlight key plot points.	Match sentences with photos.	Write a question about each photo.
	Focus for Watching	Provide story focus.	Answer questions about elements of main plot.	Answer additional questions about main plot.	Answer additional questions focused on details of story.
	After You Watch	Check story comprehension.	Answer yes/no questions about the story plot using same content as previous two exercises.	Arrange 3–6 sentences about story in proper sequence.	Add, in the appropriate place, 3–4 new sentences providing additional detail.
Language Development	*Your New Language*	Focus on language function and grammatical structure of the "Word Play" video segment, e.g., making promises: *I promise to. . ., I promise that I will. . . .*	Copy words or phrases into sentences conveying language functions.	Match 2 parts of 2-line exchanges, e.g., question-answer, statement-response.	Complete a fill-in-the-blank dialogue with correct grammatical structures.

	Exercise Section	Purpose	⭐	⭐⭐	⭐⭐⭐
	Discourse Exercise	Enable learners to see language flow.	Sequence a dialogue of 3–4 sentences.	Sequence a dialogue of 4–6 sentences.	Sequence a dialogue of 6–8 sentences.
	In Your Community	Develop reading skills using reading materials from the community, e.g., a lease.	Answer factual questions taken directly from reading.	Answer factual questions requiring synthesis.	Answer questions requiring inference.
	Read and Write	Develop reading skills	Identify main idea.	Identify factual details.	Identify tone or feeling.
		Determine meaning from context.	Identify words/phrases with same meaning.	Identify words/phrases that are clues to meaning.	Infer word meaning from text clues.
		Develop writing skills.	Provide basic factual information.	Provide additional detail.	Draw conclusions, express opinions, and other analysis, synthesis, and evaluation tasks.
Thinking Skills	*What Do You Think?*	Express and support opinions.	Indicate opinions by matching or selecting from multiple-choice items.	React to characters' opinions.	Write sentences expressing and supporting your opinions.
	Culture Clips	Recall key information presented in the *Culture Clips* video segment.	Match art with sentences from the culture clip video segment.	Complete fill-in-the-blank passage on culture clip concepts.	Respond to a situation or express an opinion related to culture clip theme.
	Check Your English	Demonstrate new material mastery.	Match written words with art depicting vocabulary.	Copy words to form a sentence/question using grammatical structure(s) presented in *Your New Language*.	Complete fill-in-the-blank passage that provides a story summary.

The *Photo Stories*

The *Photo Stories* have two primary purposes:

- They serve as a preview activity for viewers with beginning-low (but not literacy-level) English proficiency by assisting them in following the main story line when they view the video. The high-success, low-stress follow-up activities in the Photo Stories are ideal motivators for this group of learners, most of whom could not access the story without this special help.

- They can be used with learners at higher levels to preview and review the story line.

The diagram below and the descriptions that follow illustrate the carefully designed, yet simple and predictable structure of the *Photo Story* episodes.

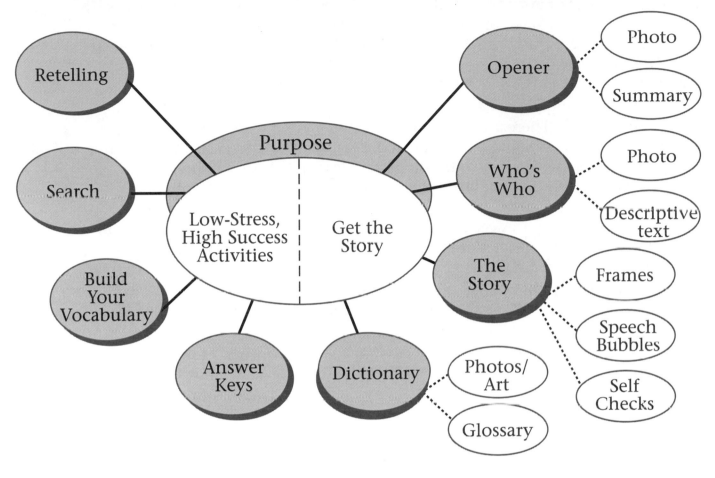

As the diagram suggests, the *Photo Stories* have a limited number of basic components, or elements:

1. **The Unit Opener:** This component helps the learner focus, using a large photo (the same one that appears at the beginning of each *Worktext* unit) that captures the theme of the episode and a capsulized summary statement of only 3 to 5 sentences that provides an overview without giving away the outcome.

2. **Who's Who:** Photos of the characters in the episode that are key to the main story line are included here. Below each photo is the character's name and a phrase describing something about the person that relates to this particular episode. For example, for Katherine in the episode "Family Matters," the phrase reads, "A single mother of two."

3. **The Story:** The story is told with photos from the episode and text, using frames and speech bubbles. Included at appropriate intervals throughout the sequence of frames are comprehension questions with which the student can self-check his or her success at "making meaning." The language "spoken" by the characters in the frames is that heard in the videos, but it is frequently simplified by deleting information, structures, and words.

4. **The Dictionary:** The dictionary provides learners with a resource for clarifying words they do not understand. It has two parts—visuals and glossary. The visuals—photos or art—may be objects, emotions, or actions that can be visually portrayed. The glossary contains six or fewer words that learners encounter in the frames. These words are not easily depicted visually and may require some explanation. The definitions given are very brief and simple. In addition, for each word in the glossary, a sentence other than the one in the video story is provided to model usage.

5. **The Activity Pages:** There are three types of activity pages—Retelling, Searches, and Build Your Vocabulary. In the Retelling activities, learners sequence pictures that represent key elements in the story. The Searches check comprehension of more detailed information, but still focus on the main theme or story line. Answers may be based on text and photo, photo only, or text only. In Build Your Vocabulary, the exercises center around a large picture that shows a scene from the story. The scene selected is rich in vocabulary that is useful to learners but not crucial to the main plot. Items in the picture are numbered, and a vocabulary list keyed to the numbers is provided. Below the pictures and vocabulary list, a series of sentences with blanks in them provides opportunities for learners to put each word into context.

6. **The Answer Keys:** The answers to all activity pages are printed upside down at the bottom of the page on which the exercise falls. The exception is the **Check Yourself** comprehension questions, whose answers are grouped together on the bottom of the first activity page.

In this way, through a well-designed combination of pictures, text, and language-learning activities, the *Photo Stories* teach basic language and reading-comprehension skills—thus propelling beginning low ESL learners toward higher levels of understanding and fluency.

Teacher's Resource Books

To help classroom teachers and distance-learning instructors give students all the help they need, each of the two *Crossroads Café Teacher's Resource Books* provides general directions for how to work with the program and specific instructions for how to use each episode. Each also has 52 reproducible master activities—4 for each of the 13 episodes in the book—for teachers to copy and give to students to complete in pairs and small groups. By working through these activities, students will be able to engage one another interactively. The following pages are examples of the type of guidance for teachers and activities for students that the *Teacher's Resource Books* provide. With these tools, teachers can make the most effective use of the *Crossroads Café* program during class time.

In Your Community

Bring to class the help wanted ads from a variety of newspapers for additional practice in reading such ads. Review them first to make sure there are ads for food servers (waiters/waitresses), bus/delivery persons, and handymen. Then do the following:

- Divide learners into mixed ability groups and distribute at least one newspaper to each group. Give each group a felt tip marker, plain white paper, scissors, and tape or glue.
- Assign each group a job classification. Ask the groups to look through their newspapers and circle all the help wanted ads for their job classification.
- Have groups compare the ads they circled to the one (for their category) in the worktext.
- Have learners cut out the ad that is most like the one in their worktexts, label it, and mount it on the plain paper.
- Have learners cut out the ads that appeal to them most, label them, and mount them on the plain paper.
- Have learners underline, with the marker, all the similarities to the worktext help wanted ad. Each group should then select one person to report to the class.

Read And Write

Visit a card shop. See how many different kinds of *I'm sorry* cards there are. Bring a few cards to class to share with the learners. Pass the cards around or make overhead transparencies before learners write the note in the worktext. Also remind learners they do not have to share anything too personal. If they cannot think of a note of apology, they can make up something.

If possible, replay the video scenes below that feature Jess and Carol before learners complete the writing activities in the worktext.

Counter Times	Scenes
01:65–02:29	Carol gives Jess a watch.
04:15–05:08	Jess and Carol argue about going out for dinner.
08:05–08:60	Carol comes to the café to talk to Jess.

Extension Activity #1 is a large group discussion about making apologies.

- Talk about Jess and Carol's arguments in the video—the watch and going out for dinner. Talk about Jess's note to Carol.
- Ask learners what they do when they are sorry or want to apologize for something. Tell them:
  Raise your hand if you ever say you're sorry.
  Raise your hand if you ever write a note to say you're sorry.
  Raise your hand if you ever send flowers to say you're sorry.
- Ask learners about other things they do when they apologize. Write them down for everyone to see. If you observe any gender or cultural patterns, point them out and ask the learners to comment.

Extension Activity #2 is a roleplay. Prepare situation cards such as the ones below. Here are some suggestions:

- You're late to class (student/teacher).
- You forgot to meet your friend for lunch (friend/friend).
- You forgot to tell your spouse you'd be home late (wife/husband).
- You forgot your friend's birthday (friend/friend).
- You were playing music too loud (neighbor/neighbor).

A variation is to have learners think of situations with a partner and write them on blank 3" × 5" cards. Collect the cards. Ask for volunteers to roleplay each situation. Each pair picks a card at random and decides which roles each will play.

What Do You Think?

The employees traded jobs and Carol and Jess traded roles. After learners complete this page in the worktext, have them do a three-step interview on the theme of the unit—Trading Places. Ask the following questions.

Handout 13-A

Work with a partner. One person is A and the other is B. Work together to complete the grid below.

1. In the *top left-hand box*, write **four** things you both can do well.
2. In the *top right-hand box*, write **four** things A can do but B can't.
3. In the *bottom left-hand box* write **four** things B can do but A can't.
4. In the *bottom right-hand box* write **four** things neither of you can do well.

Both A and B	Only A
Only B	**Neither A nor B**

The Crossroads Café Partner's Guide

The *Partner's Guide* is a small book—just 32 pages—that a formal tutor, a relative, a friend, a coworker, or a neighbor can use to help a learner improve his or her English. This little guide explains, in simple, direct language, what the "helper" can do to make learning with each episode of *Crossroads Café* even better for the student. The guide provides one page of special instructions for each episode, as well as some general suggestions for a predictable yet lively approach to working with the learner. People who have never taught and seasoned tutors will find a wealth of hints in the *Tutor's Guide* for helping students succeed with their English.

The Crossroads Café Reproducible Master Packet

For the tutor who is working with more than one learner of *Crossroads Café*, the same 104 reproducible masters that are part of the *Teacher's Resource Books* are available separately. The masters can also be used by tutors who want to maximize a single learner's opportunities for interaction by working through the communicative activities in a learning-partner role with the student.

Unit 1: Opening Day

Before You Watch (page 3)

○ <u>3</u> application form <u>4</u> fire extinguisher
 <u>6</u> backpack <u>1</u> restaurant
 <u>2</u> chef <u>5</u> tools

○○ <u>5</u> The handyman repairs something.
 <u>2</u> The chef becomes angry and quits.
 <u>1</u> The owner watches workers prepare his restaurant for opening day.
 <u>3</u> The owner gives an application form to one of the applicants.
 <u>6</u> The owner puts food in a teenager's backpack.
 <u>4</u> Two people try to put out a fire.

After You Watch (pages 4 and 5)

○ 1. c 2. a 3. d

○○ 1. b 2. f

○○○ 1. e

○ 1. no 2. yes 3. no 4. yes

○○ <u>2</u> The chef quits.
 <u>1</u> Mr. Brashov is opening a restaurant.
 <u>4</u> He needs to hire a waitress too.
 <u>3</u> He needs to hire a new chef.

○○○ Mr. Brashov is opening a restaurant. There's a problem with the stove. The chef quits. He asks Jamal to fix the stove. He needs to hire a new chef. He hires Rosa because she makes a delicious dessert. He needs to hire a waitress, too.

Your New Language (pages 6 and 7)

○ 1. Jess Washington Mississippi
 2. Victor Brashov Romania
 3. Jamal Al-Jibali Egypt
 4. Rosa Rivera Mexico

○○ 1. c 2. e 3. a 4. b 5. d

○○○ 1. am 4. He 7. he
 2. you 5. his 8. from
 3. was 6. is

(page 8)

○ <u>4</u> HENRY: Henry Chang
 <u>2</u> HENRY: Yes?
 <u>1</u> MR. BRASHOV: Excuse me, young man.
 <u>3</u> MR. BRASHOV: What is your name?

○○ <u>3</u> ROSA: I am Rosa Rivera
 <u>1</u> ROSA: I am looking for Mr. Brashov.
 <u>4</u> MR. BRASHOV: Where are you from?
 <u>2</u> MR. BRASHOV: I am Mr. Brashov. Who are you?
 <u>5</u> ROSA: I was born in this country, but I grew up in Mexico.

_4_ **JESS:**	I used to work for the post office. Now I'm retired.
_2_ **MR. BRASHOV:**	Victor Brashov.
_3_ **MR. BRASHOV:**	What do you do for a living, Jess?
_6_ **JESS:**	Is that so?
_1_ **JESS:**	The name is Jess. Jess Washington.
_5_ **MR. BRASHOV:**	I used to be retired. Now I own this restaurant!

In Your Community (page 9)

○ 1. Anne   2. waitress   3. June 1985

○○ 1. Katherine hasn't worked since June 1985.
   2. She has five years experience.

○○○   It might not be easy for Katherine to get a job because she hasn't worked for more than ten years. It might be easy for Katherine to get a job because she hasn't had recent experience, so an employer can hire her for less money.

Read and Write (page 10)

Circle the Answers

○ b

○○ b

○○○ b

Find the Word

○ b

○○ a

○○○ c

Culture Clip (page 13)

○ 1. b   2. c   3. a

○○ 1. rules   5. questions
   2. job   6. eye contact
   3. handshake   7. confident
   4. alert

Check Your English (page 14)

○ 1. tools   3. application form   5. fire extinguisher
  2. chef   4. backpack   6. restaurant

○○ 1. Mr. Brashov's first name is Victor. OR Is Mr. Brashov's first name Victor?
   2. Where is Rosa from?
   3. Henry is from China. OR Is Henry from China?
   4. What is Katherine's last name?

○○○ 1. owner   7. hires
    2. problems   8. applicant
    3. chef   9. handyman
    4. waiter   10. freezer
    5. name   11. directions
    6. waitress   12. delivery

Unit 2: Growing Pains

Before You Watch (page 16)

- **5** work-study form
- **2** customer
- **3** birthday cake
- **6** violin
- **4** parents
- **1** health and safety inspector

- **6** The woman is holding a violin case. She looks angry.
- **4** Mr. Brashov is shaking hands with a man.
- **2** Mr. Brashov and Henry are talking with a customer.
- **1** Mr. Brashov is talking to a woman who has some papers in her hand.
- **3** Someone in Henry's family is having a birthday party.
- **5** Henry and Mr. Brashov are in the office with Henry's parents.

After You Watch (pages 18 and 19)

◑ 1. g.　　2. b　　3. h

◐◐ 1. f　　2. e　　3. d

◐◐◐ 1. a　　2. c

◑ 1. No　2. Yes　3. Yes　4. No　5. Yes

◐◐ **6** At first, they tell Henry that he cannot work. When they see Henry's violin they change their minds.
- **4** Henry has not told his family that he works at Crossroads Café.
- **3** Henry's Uncle Fred stops by for some pie and is surprised to see Henry.
- **2** She is not the only unexpected visitor.
- **5** When his parents discover that Henry is working, they are very angry.
- **1** One afternoon, the health and safety inspector arrives unexpectedly to inspect Crossroads Café.

◐◐◐　　One afternoon, the health and safety inspector arrives unexpectedly to inspect Crossroads Café. She is there to make sure that the café has no health and safety violations. She is not the only unexpected visitor. Henry's Uncle Fred stops by for some pie and is surprised to see Henry. Henry is surprised too. Henry is upset to see his uncle because he has not told his family that he works at Crossroads Café. In fact, he has lied to Mr. Brashov and signed his father's name on the work-study form. When his parents discover that Henry is working, they are very angry. At first, they tell Henry that he cannot work. When they see Henry's violin, they change their minds. They decide that Henry must prove that he can work at Crossroads Café and keep up with his school work and violin lessons.

Your New Language (pages 20 and 21)

◑ 1. the health inspector
3. too

2. the owner, Henry's uncle
4. Henry's mother

◐◐ 1. b　　2. d　　3. c　　4. a　　5. c

◐◐◐ 1. I'm
2. It's nice to meet you.
3. I'm Victor Brashov.

4. the cook
5. It's a pleasure to meet both of you.
6. this is

7. the handyman
8. Glad to meet you.
9. Glad to meet you, too.

(page 22)

◑ **2** ROSA:　　　　Oh, nice to meet you. I'm Rosa, the cook.
- **1** UNCLE FRED:　Hi, I'm Henry's uncle, Fred.
- **4** ROSA:　　　　Yes. I'll get him.
- **3** UNCLE FRED:　Nice to meet you, too. Is Henry here?

∞	4	JESS:	It's a pleasure to meet you. Henry's such a great boy.
	2	JESS:	Fine, Henry. How are things with you?
	1	HENRY:	Hi, Jess, how are you?
	3	HENRY:	O.K. Jess, this is my Mom and Dad, Mr. and Mrs. Chang. Mom and Dad this is Jess.
	5	CHANGS:	Thank you. It's a pleasure to meet you also.
∞∞	3	YOU:	Not bad, thanks. Rosa, this is Bill Jones, my neighbor. Rosa Rivera, this is Bill Jones.
	1	YOU:	Hi, Rosa. How are you?
	4	B:	Nice to meet you.
	2	A:	Fine, thanks. How are you?
	5	C:	Nice to meet you too, Rosa.
	6	YOU:	Bill, Rosa is a great cook. Wait until you try her special today.

In Your Community (page 23)

✪ 1. no   2. no

✪✪ 1. no   2. no

Read and Write (page 24)

Circle the Answers

✪ b

✪✪ c

✪✪✪ c

Find the Word

✪ a

✪✪ b

✪✪✪ b

Culture Clip (page 27)

✪ 1. c   2. b   3. a

✪✪ 1. children   4. decisions   7. richness
    2. independent   5. family
    3. ages   6. balance

Check Your English (page 28)

✪ 1. health and safety inspector   3. birthday cake   5. work study form
    2. customer   4. parents   6. violin

✪✪ 1. Jamal, this is Ms. Reilly, the health inspector.
    2. It's nice to meet you.
    3. Nice to meet you too.
    4. Ms. Reilly, this is Jamal, our handyman.

✪✪✪ 1. inspector   5. program   8. signature
    2. visitor   6. parents   9. form
    3. surprised   7. angry   10. prove
    4. job

Unit 3: Worlds Apart

Before You Watch (page 30)

    ❂ 4 flowers   2 shawl
         6 pillow   5 plan
         3 roommate   1 suitcase

    ❂❂ 4 The man brings Rosa flowers.
         6 Brashov receives a package.
         5 The Rosa shows her plans to the man.
         1 A man comes to visit.
         2 The man gives Rosa a necklace.
         3 Rosa introduces the man to her roommate.

After You Watch (pages 32 and 33)

    ❂ 1. d   2. b   3. a

    ❂❂ 1. e   2. c

    ❂❂❂ 1. f   2. c

    ❂ 1. yes   2. yes   3. no   4. no

    ❂❂ 4 Rosa decides not to go back to Mexico.
         1 Miguel comes to visit Rosa.
         2 Miguel asks Rosa to marry him.
         3 Rosa shows Miguel her plans for a restaurant.

    ❂❂❂   Miguel comes to visit Rosa. Miguel brings Rosa a present from home. Miguel asks Rosa to marry him. Rosa makes plans for a restaurant in Puebla. Rosa shows Miguel her plans for a restaurant. Miguel doesn't think Rosa's restaurant will be a success in Puebla. Rosa decides not to go back to Mexico.

Your New Language (pages 34 and 35)

    ❂ 1. to marry you
       2. to surprise me
       3. something to drink?
       4. an international menu

    ❂❂ 1. c   2. a   3. b   4. e   5. d

    ❂❂❂ 1. want to   5. want to
          2. want   6. want
          3. don't want   7. want
          4. want to   8. don't want to

(page 36)

    ❂ 2 MRS. GILROY: We want two orders of Monterey Chicken.
       1 KATHERINE: Yes, Mrs. Gilroy. Can I help you?
       3 KATHERINE: Do you want something to drink?

    ❂❂ 4 CARRIE: What do you want to do? Get married or open a restaurant?
       3 ROSA: I don't know. He wants to help me open a restaurant in Puebla.
       5 ROSA: I don't know.
       1 ROSA: Miguel wants me to marry him.
       2 CARRIE: That's great. Isn't it?

⊙⊙⊙ _2_ MIGUEL: Rosa . . . this is wonderful. The names is "Around the World?"

    _5_ ROSA: Did you see the way I want to arrange things? I want to have the kitchen in the same room as the customers.

    _1_ ROSA: Here. Let me show you my plans for a restaurant in Puebla.

    _4_ MIGUEL: I'm not sure an international restaurant would be a success in Puebla.

    _3_ ROSA: Yes. I want to serve great dishes from around the world. These are some menu ideas.

    _6_ MIGUEL: Wait a minute, Rosa. People don't want to watch the food being cooked.

In Your Community (page 37)

❂ 1. 753-0142
2. 451-HAIR
3. 924 Lincoln

❂❂ 1. the Truck Driver Training School and the Western Career College
2. restaurant management training

❂❂❂ the American Business Academy because the class she is taking is a business class.

Read and Write (page 38)

Circle the Answers

  ❂ b

 ❂❂ a

❂❂❂ c

Find the Word

  ❂ c

 ❂❂ a

❂❂❂ b

Culture Clip (page 41)

❂ 1. c   2. a   3. b

❂❂ 1. century   4. controlled   7. freedom
2. survive   5. reasons   8. opportunity
3. immigration   6. immigrants

Check Your English (page 42)

❂ 1. pillow   3. necklace   5. suitcase
2. flowers   4. plan   6. roommate

❂❂ 1. What do you want to eat?
2. I want the chicken.
3. I want you to come home.
4. Rosa doesn't want to go back home.

❂❂❂ 1. visit   5. open   9. kitchen
2. marry   6. plans   10. people
3. wants   7. menu   11. different
4. restaurant   8. international   12. go back

Unit 4: Who's the Boss

Before You Watch (page 44)

✪ _6_ newspaper   _2_ glasses
    _4_ wires   _1_ coffee pot
    _3_ menu   _5_ notebook

✪✪ _5_ The man writes as he talks to Jamal.
    _3_ Two men look at menus.
    _6_ Jess reads a newspaper article.
    _4_ Jamal is fixing something.
    _2_ Jamal and Jihan go to a party.
    _1_ Jess looks angry as he talks to Katherine.

After You Watch (pages 46 and 47)

✪ 1. e   2. d   3. b

✪✪ 1. a   2. c

✪✪✪ 1. c   2. a

✪ 1. no   2. yes   3. yes   4. yes

✪✪ _3_ Abdullah and Mohammed go to see Jamal at Crossroads Café.
    _1_ Jamal sees his friends, Abdullah and Mohammed at a party.
    _2_ Jamal can't tell his friends that he is only a handyman.
    _4_ At the café, Jamal pretends that he is the boss.

✪✪✪   Jamal sees his friends, Abdullah and Mohammed, at a party. When they meet him, they ask him about his job. Jamal can't tell his friends that he is only a handyman. Jamal tells them he is in the restaurant business. Abdullah and Mohammed go to see Jamal at Crossroads Café. At the café, Jamal pretends that he is the boss. After awhile, Jamal finally tells his friends that he is the handyman and not the boss.

Your New Language (pages 48 and 49)

✪ 1. forgot
   2. couldn't
   3. called
   4. talked

✪✪ 1. b   2. d   3. a   4. c

✪✪✪ 1. that   5. telling
    2. lied   6. sorry
    3. sorry   7. lying
    4. felt

(page 50)

✪ _3_ JAMAL: I told you I was the owner. But I am only the handyman.
    _2_ ABDULLAH: How? What did you say?
    _4_ ABDULLAH: Don't worry, Jamal. We like you for who you are.
    _1_ JAMAL: I'm sorry that I lied.

⊙⊙ _3_ JAMAL:	But Mr. Brashov, I have another question to ask you.	
_5_ JAMAL:	Yes, I guess so. We can talk later.	
_1_ JAMAL:	Mr. Brashov, can I talk with you for a moment?	
_2_ MR. BRASHOV:	I'm sorry, Jamal. I can't talk to you right now.	
_4_ MR. BRASHOV:	Can it wait until later? First I need to finish the supply list.	
⊙⊙⊙ _3_ MR. BRASHOV:	I don't want to talk here. Let's go to the back room. Then we can have some privacy.	
_6_ JESS:	No, I don't think so. My hearing is just fine.	
_1_ MR. BRASHOV:	Can I talk to you for a minute, my friend?	
_5_ MR. BRASHOV:	Jess, I think you may have a hearing problem.	
_2_ JESS:	What do you want to talk about?	
_7_ MR. BRASHOV:	I'm sorry, Jess, I don't think it is. Maybe you should have it checked.	
_4_ JESS:	O.K. Now we are alone. What do you want to say?	

In Your Community (page 51)

⊙ 1. Middletown   2. $ 6.95 per person   3. Monday   4. 7:00 a.m.

⊙⊙ 1. No   2. Sometimes   3. Yes

⊙⊙⊙ 1. Yes   2. Yes. Delivery is free only if your order is more than $10.00.

Read and Write (page 52)

Circle the Answers

⊙ b   **⊙⊙** a   **⊙⊙⊙** c

Find the Word

⊙ b   **⊙⊙** a   **⊙⊙⊙** a

Culture Clip (page 55)

⊙ 1. c   2. d   3. a   4. b

⊙⊙ 1. jobs   6. industries   11. occupations
2. reasons   7. retraining   12. experiences
3. countries   8. programs   13. beginning
4. home   9. support
5. laid off   10. difficult

Check Your English (page 56)

⊙ 1. coffee pot   3. glass   5. notebook
2. menu   4. wires   6. newspaper

⊙⊙ 1. I'm sorry that I didn't tell the truth.
2. We're sorry for coming late to your party.
3. I'm sorry that I couldn't fix the alarm.
4. I'm sorry for making a mess in the kitchen.

⊙⊙⊙ 1. job   7. pretends
2. engineer   8. feels
3. handyman   9. tells
4. restaurant   10. friends
5. boss   11. successful
6. helps

Unit 5: Lost and Found

Before You Watch (page 59)

✪ _6_ neighbors   _2_ police officer
   _4_ security devices   _1_ burglary
   _5_ alarm system   _3_ salesperson

✪✪ _3_ A man is showing a security device to Jess and Carol.
   _6_ The neighbors come to Carol's house.
   _4_ There are many security devices on the table.
   _1_ There has been a burglary at Carol and Jess's home.
   _5_ Jamal is helping Jess.
   _2_ The police officer is talking to Carol and Jess.

After You Watch (pages 60 and 61)

✪ 1. c   2. d

✪✪ 1. a   2. e.

✪✪✪ 1. b.

✪ 1. yes   2. no   3. no   4. yes

✪✪ _4_ Jess doesn't buy any devices because they are too expensive.
   _2_ A police officer comes and takes a crime report.
   _5_ Carol and the neighbors meet to discuss crime prevention in their neighborhood.
   _1_ There is a burglary at Jess and Carol's house.
   _3_ Jess has a salesperson come to show him security devices.

✪✪✪   There is a burglary at Jess and Carol's house. A police officer comes and takes a crime report. They ask for a description of the items that were stolen. Jess has a salesman come to show him security devices. Jess doesn't buy any devices because they are too expensive. He buys a do-it-yourself alarm kit and asks Jamal to help him. The alarm system does not work. Carol and the neighbors meet to discuss crime prevention in their neighborhood.

Your New Language (pages 62 and 63)

✪ 1. the ball
   2. out of here
   3. the blue wire
   4. ears

✪✪ 1. d.   2. a   3. e   4. b   5. c

✪✪✪ 1. come   6. talk
   2. do   7. don't be
   3. clean   8. keep
   4. set   9. Don't make
   5. Do not leave

(page 64)

✪ _3_ JOSH: Oh, O.K. Give me the ball, please.
   _1_ JOSH: Come on, mister. Give me the ball!
   _2_ MR. BRASHOV: I will not give you the ball until you say, please.

∞	_3_ JAMAL:	You can come in in a few minutes. Please, cover your ears. It will be very loud.
	_1_ JAMAL:	Mrs. Washington, go outside and close the door. I'll set the alarm.
	_2_ CAROL:	O.K. Let me know when I can come in.
	_4_ CAROL:	I will. Knock when you're ready.
∞∞	_5_ CAROL:	It's very heavy. But, steel bars remind me of jail.
	_3_ JESS:	Sure. Carol, move the plants and I'll get the lamp.
	_2_ SALESPERSON:	I have several security devices. I'll need to use your table to lay them all out.
	_4_ SALESPERSON:	Thanks. This is perfect. Pick up the steel bar, Mrs. Washington. What do you think?
	_6_ SALESPERSON:	If you don't like the bars, then install one of these alarm systems. Take a look at this one. It includes a closed-circuit camera.
	_1_ JESS:	Thanks for coming, Mr. Kincaid. What can you show us?

In Your Community (page 65)

❂ 1. yes   2. yes

❂❂ 1. no   2. yes

❂❂❂ 1. yes   2. yes

Read and Write (page 66)

Circle the Answers

❂ 1. b   ❂❂ 1. a   ❂❂❂ 1. c

Find the Word

❂ 1. jewelry   2. upset

❂❂ 1. unfortunate   2. note

❂❂❂ 1. gather   2. break in

Culture Clip (page 69)

❂ 1. c   3. b
   2. d   4. a

❂❂ 1. neighbors   6. police
   2. prevent   7. protect
   3. report   8. community
   4. graffiti
   5. meetings

Check Your English (page 70)

❂ 1. burglary   3. salesperson   5. alarm system
   2. police officer   4. security devices   6. neighbors

❂❂ 1. Push the button and cover your ears.
   2. Please be quiet and sit down!
   3. Lock the doors and the windows.
   4. Please don't stay out late at night.

❂❂❂ 1. burglary   5. security devices   9. meeting
   2. burglars   6. price   10. prevention
   3. crime report   7. expensive
   4. salesperson   8. install

Unit 6: Time is Money

Before You Watch (page 72)

✪ _2_ business card   _3_ telephone (or 4)
_5_ chart   _6_ trophy
_1_ paperwork   _4_ watch (or 3)

✪✪ _6_ The man leaves with a trophy.
_3_ A man times Katherine with a watch.
_1_ Mr. Brashov has a lot of paperwork.
_5_ The man talks about a chart.
_2_ Jess gives Mr. Brashov a business card.
_4_ The man writes and Mr. Brashov talks on the phone.

After You Watch (pages 74 and 75)

✪ 1. c   2. f

✪✪ 1. e   2. a

✪✪ 1. d   2. b

✪ 1. no   2. no   3. yes   4. no

✪✪ _2_ Emery Bradford helps Mr. Brashov organize his paperwork.
_1_ Mr. Brashov has too much paperwork.
_4_ Mr. Brashov does not like the changes or the contest.
_3_ Mr. Bradford has a contest for the most efficient employee.

✪✪✪   Mr. Brashov has too much paperwork. He has too many bills and too many receipts. Emery Bradford helps Mr. Brashov organize his paperwork. He wants to make people work faster. Mr. Bradford has a contest for the most efficient employee. Mr. Brashov does not like the changes or the contest. When Mr. Bradford leaves, Mr. Brashov and his employees are happy.

Your New Language (pages 76 and 77)

✪ 1. take off your headphones?
2. go to the library?
3. have another cup?
4. make a schedule?

✪✪ 1. b   2. a   3. e   4. c   5. d

✪✪✪ 1. How about   2. Why don't you   3. Maybe you should   4. How about

(page 78)

✪ _1_ We need a new filter.
_3_ Filters are cheaper at Bidwell's Hardware.
_2_ Why don't you get one at Joe's Hardware?

✪✪ _4_ I still need to have a way to know when to pay them.
_2_ Good. I need help.
_3_ First, you should divide your bills into categories—rent, supplies, utlities.
_1_ I'll help you organize your paperwork.
_5_ How about using this calendar to make a schedule?

⊗⊗⊗ _3_ But they might be sold out.
  _5_ One last suggestion. Why don't you leave your headphones at home?
  _2_ Maybe you should buy them after work instead of before work.
  _1_ I'm sorry I'm late. I was buying tickets for a concert.
  _5_ O.K. Next time I'll call.
  _4_ And another thing. How about calling if you're going to be late!

In Your Community (page 79)

⊗ 1. Monday
  2. at 6:30 P.M.
  3. at 7:50 P.M.

⊗⊗ 1. 1 hour and 20 minutes
  2. 3 times a week
  3. 5 hours a week

⊗⊗⊗ 1. No, because they are both on Monday evening at about the same time.

Read and Write (page 80)

Circle the Answers

  ⊗ c

  ⊗⊗ a

⊗⊗⊗ c

Find the Word

  ⊗ disorganized

  ⊗⊗ organize

⊗⊗⊗ normal

Culture Clip (page 83)

  ⊗ 1. b   2. c   3. a
  ⊗⊗ 1. business   4. needs   7. appointment
    2. sports   5. late   8. ticket
    3. time   6. lose

Check Your English (page 84)

  ⊗ 1. trophy   3. chart   5. telephone
    2. paperwork   4. watch   6. business card

  ⊗⊗ 1. Maybe you should go to the library.
    2. How about getting a study partner?
    3. Why don't you make a schedule?
    4. Maybe you should get help.

  ⊗⊗⊗ 1. paperwork   5. save   9. can't
    2. him   6. He   10. belong
    3. bills   7. most   11. Emery
    4. change   8. is

Unit 7: Fish Out of Water

Before You Watch (page 86)

✪ <u>5</u> poster <u>2</u> handkerchief
<u>3</u> flag <u>1</u> banner
<u>4</u> band <u>6</u> wallet

✪✪ <u>5</u> There is a poster on the wall.
<u>6</u> A man gives a wallet to Mr. Brashov.
<u>1</u> Jamal hangs a banner in the café.
<u>4</u> Mr. Brashov is angry with some men in the café.
<u>2</u> Mr. Brashov sneezes into a handkerchief.
<u>3</u> There is a flag above the kitchen door.

After You Watch (pages 88 and 89)

✪ 1. d 2. a 3. e

✪✪ 1. a 2. b

✪✪✪ 1. d 2. c

✪ 1. no 2. no 3. no 4. no

✪✪ <u>2</u> He wants to learn about the café so he can help Mr. Brashov.
<u>1</u> Mr. Brashov's brother Nicolae comes to visit from Romania.
<u>4</u> Then Nicolae leaves the United States and goes back to Romania.
<u>3</u> While Mr. Brashov is at home, Nicolae makes some changes in the café.

✪✪✪ Mr. Brashov's brother comes to visit from Romania. He wants to learn about the café so he can help Mr. Brashov. When Mr. Brashov becomes sick, Nicolae takes charge of the café. While Mr. Brashov is at home, Nicolae makes some changes in the café. When Mr. Brashov returns and sees what Nicolae has done, he becomes angry. The two brothers argue and Nicolae leaves the café. Then Nicolae leaves the United States and goes back to Romania.

Your New Language (pages 90 and 91)

✪ 1. learned
2. recovered
3. warmed
4. worked

✪✪ 1. d. 2. b 3. a 4. e 5. c

✪✪✪ 1. brought 4. tried
2. done 5. have
3. have learned 6. eaten

(page 92)

✪ <u>4</u> NICOLAE: He's planning to come in tomorrow.
<u>2</u> NICOLAE: Better. He has recovered from the flu.
<u>3</u> KATHERINE: That's good news. When can he come back to work?
<u>1</u> KATHERINE: So, how is Mr. Brashov?

✪✪ <u>5</u> NICOLAE: I'm sorry, but I have worked very hard to make the café more like home. I thought it would please you.
<u>1</u> NICOLAE: Ah, Victor. Welcome back. We have missed you.
<u>3</u> NICOLAE: But, Victor, they have played for only a short time.

<u>2</u> MR. BRASHOV:	Nicolae, what is going on here? Make them stop!	
<u>4</u> MR. BRASHOV:	I don't care how long they have played! This is not a dance hall. Why have you done this to my café?	

<u>2</u> MR. BRASHOV: Nicolae, what is going on here? Make them stop!

<u>4</u> MR. BRASHOV: I don't care how long they have played! This is not a dance hall. Why have you done this to my café?

✪✪✪ <u>5</u> ROSA: I have been here for five years and it never feels like home.

<u>4</u> MR. BRASHOV: Not like it? That is not possible. This is the United States. This could have been his home.

<u>2</u> MR. BRASHOV: No, I'm not all right. For a long time I have wanted Nicolae to live in the United States with me. Now he has gone back home to Romania.

<u>3</u> ROSA: Maybe he did not like it here.

<u>1</u> ROSA: Are you all right, Mr. Brashov?

<u>6</u> MR. BRASHOV: Maybe you're right. Maybe Nicolae never felt at home here and the best place for him is Romania. But I will miss him.

In Your Community (page 93)

✪ 1. Romanian Noodles with Garlic Sauce   2. 1 lb.

✪✪ 1. 6   2. You make the garlic sauce.

✪✪✪ 1. No, you will not have enough food for everyone at your dinner. This recipe serves only 6 people.
2. No, These are ingredients you can find at most stores. There are no Romanian ingredients listed in the recipe.

Read and Write (page 94)

Circle the Answers

✪ c   ✪✪ a   ✪✪✪ b

Find the Word

✪ b   ✪✪ c   ✪✪✪ a

Culture Clip (page 97)

✪ 1. b   2. d   3. a   4. c

✪✪ 1. country   4. newcomers   7. language
2. exciting   5. lonely   8. comfortable
3. journey   6. customs

Check Your English (page 98)

✪ 1. flag   3. band   5. picture
2. banner   4. poster   6. handkerchief

✪✪ 1. Jamal has fixed the stove. OR Has Jamal fixed the stove?
2. You have learned to play chess very well. OR Have you learned to play chess very well?
3. Rosa has been in the United States for five years. OR Has Rosa been in the United States for five years?
4. How long has Nicolae lived in Romania?

✪✪✪ 1. has   6. angry   10. wallet
2. café   7. done   11. home
3. sick   8. mall   12. visited
4. supply list   9. gift   13. stay
5. band

Unit 8: Family Matters

Before You Watch (page 100)

- ✪ _2_ catalogue   _3_ TV remote control
  _4_ drawing   _5_ model plane
  _6_ people hugging   _1_ a person yawning

- ✪✪ _4_ Katherine's daughter shows Rosa a drawing.
  _2_ Katherine and Jamal look at a catalogue.
  _3_ Katherine's children fight about the TV.
  _5_ David brings Jess's model airplane to the café.
  _1_ Jess and Mr. Brashov worry about Katherine.
  _6_ Katherine is happy to see her children.

After You Watch (pages 102 and 103)

- ✪ 1. d   2. d   3. b

- ✪✪ 1. a   2. c

- ✪✪✪ 1. a   2. b

- ✪ 1. yes   2. no   3. no   4. yes

- ✪✪ _2_ Rosa finds out Katherine has a second job.
  _1_ The workers at Crossroads Café worry about Katherine.
  _3_ Katherine sees Suzanne's drawing.
  _4_ Katherine takes her children to the lake.

- ✪✪✪   Katherine is very tired. The people at Crossroads Café worry about Katherine. Rosa finds out Katherine has a second job. Suzanne draws a picture of two unhappy children. Katherine finds Suzanne at home without David. Katherine sees Suzanne's drawing. Katherine takes her children to the lake.

Your New Language (pages 104 and 105)

- ✪ 1. show you how
  2. fix dinner
  3. help you do it
  4. babysit

- ✪✪ 1. d   2. c   3. e   4. b   5. a

- ✪✪✪ 1. Would you like me to   4. Would you like me to
  2. I'll   5. I'll
  3. I'll   6. I'll

(page 106)

- ✪ _3_ KATHERINE: Thank you.
  _2_ JAMAL: You're right. I'll turn up the heat.
  _1_ KATHERINE: It's too cold in here.

- ✪✪ _2_ KATHERINE: The house is a mess!
  _1_ DAVID: What's wrong?
  _4_ KATHERINE: Good idea. You clean the house and I'll cook dinner.
  _3_ DAVID: Would you like me to clean it?

__4_ JAMAL: Would you like me to look at it?
   __2_ JAMAL: What kind of trouble?
   __6_ JAMAL: I hope we don't have to do that. They're expensive.
   __1_ MR. BRASHOV: I'm having trouble with the thermostat.
   __5_ MR. BRASHOV: Please. And then if you can't fix it, I'll call a repair person.
   __3_ MR. BRASHOV: I can't get the on/off switch to move.

In Your Community (page 107)

✪ 1. #61917
   2. $1,799.99

✪✪ 1. $2,766.94
   2. One is 650 MB, and one is 850 MB.

✪✪✪ 1. the printer
   2. The total cost of the separate components is $2,766.94. The complete system + printer is
$2,099.98. It is $666.96 less to buy the system and printer than to buy the components separately.

Read and Write (page 108)

Circle the Answers

  ✪ c   ✪✪ b   ✪✪✪ a

Find the Word

  ✪ lie   ✪✪ drawing   ✪✪✪ luxury

Culture Clip (page 111)

✪ 1. c   2. d   3. a   4. b

✪✪ 1. families   5. pulled
   2. concern   6. earn
   3. financial   7. separated
   4. children   8. hard

Check Your English (page 112)

✪ 1. yawn   3. hug   5. drawing
   2. model airplane   4. catalogue   6. TV remote control

✪✪ 1. I'll teach you to dance.
   2. I'll help you with your homework.
   3. Would you like me to mail your letters?
   4. Would you like me to help you decorate?

✪✪✪ 1. computer   5. tired   9. homework
   2. money   6. late   10. together
   3. problems   7. babysit   11. drawing
   4. worry   8. friends   12. more

Unit 9: Rush to Judgment

Before You Watch (page 114)

☼ _3_ patrol car   _1_ license plate
   _2_ toolbox   _4_ police officer
   _5_ handcuffs   _6_ police station

☼☼ _5_ Jamal has handcuffs on his wrists.
   _3_ There are two men in a car.
   _6_ Mr. Brashov walks out of the police station with Jamal.
   _1_ Jamal picks up his tools.
   _4_ Two men talk to Mr. Brashov.
   _2_ A man pushes Jamal against the car.

After You Watch (pages 116 and 117)

☼ 1. d   2. c.   3. b

☼☼ 1. a   2. a   3. f

☼☼☼ 1. e   2. g

☼ 1. No   2. Yes   3. Yes   4. No

☼☼ _3_ Mr. Brashov comes to the police station to help Jamal.
   _1_ The police see Jamal on the street with his toolbox.
   _2_ The police do not believe Jamal and take him to the police station in handcuffs.
   _4_ The officers finally believe Jamal and tell him that he can leave.

☼☼☼   The police see Jamal on the street with his toolbox. The officers want to know why Jamal has a lot of tools. The police do not believe Jamal and take him to the police station in handcuffs. Jamal has to answer many questions at the police station. Jamal makes a phone call to Crossroads Café to ask for help. Mr. Brashov comes to the police station to help Jamal. The officers finally believe Jamal and tell him that he can leave.

Your New Language (pages 118 and 119)

☼ 1. gray   2. brown hair   3. missing   4. bad   5. innocent

☼☼ 1. b   2. d   3. e   4. c   5. a

☼☼☼ 1. tired   5. dark hairt
   2. sick   6. medium build
   3. suspect   7. innocent
   4. twenties   8. wrong

(page 120)

☼ _4_ BENTON: No, she is with a white male in his mid thirties.
   _3_ ANDERSON: Is she alone?
   _2_ BENTON: She is tall with long, brown hair.
   _1_ ANDERSON: What does our suspect look like?

☼☼ _2_ JESS: Don't worry, Henry, we'll find them. What do they look like?
   _4_ JESS: How about your grandfather?
   _3_ HENRY: My grandmother is five feet tall with gray hair.
   _1_ HENRY: My grandparents are missing.
   _6_ JESS: Let's go look for them. I'll give you a ride in my car.
   _5_ HENRY: His hair is a little gray, too. He is about five feet five inches tall, has a slim build, and wears glasses.

⬤⬤⬤	_4_ JESS:	There is something about burglaries here in the newspaper. The suspect is a male in his late twenties with a medium build and short dark hair.
	_3_ MR. BRASHOV:	To question him. Something about some burglaries.
	_5_ MR. BRASHOV:	That sounds like a description of Jamal, doesn't it?
	_1_ MR. BRASHOV:	The police took Jamal to the police station.
	_7_ MR. BRASHOV:	I hope the police know it, too.
	_6_ JESS:	Yes, it does. But I know Jamal wasn't involved in any of this.
	_2_ JESS:	Why?

In Your Community (page 121)

⬤ 1. 17 Cummings St. Apt #2, Middletown   2. 150 lbs.   3. El-Bially   4. 5 feet 7 inches

⬤⬤ 1. No, because the report says that Jamal did not have any weapons.
   2. No, because it says he was born in Cairo, Egypt.

⬤⬤⬤ 1. No, because Jamal does not have a large build and does not have blond hair.
   2. The report says that Jamal wears glasses. Jamal doesn't wear glasses.

Read and Write (page 122)

Circle the Answers

⬤ b   ⬤⬤ a   ⬤⬤⬤ c

Find the Word

⬤ a   ⬤⬤ b   ⬤⬤⬤ b

Culture Clip (page 125)

⬤ 1. b   2. a   3. c

⬤⬤
1. public	4. friendly	7. arresting	10. jail
2. children	5. merchants	8. tickets	11. police officer
3. community	6. happening	9. crime	

Check Your English (page 126)

⬤
| 1. license plate | 3. patrol car | 5. police station |
| 2. toolbox | 4. handcuffs | 6. police officer |

⬤⬤ 1. Jamal is an innocent man. OR Is Jamal an innocent man?
   2. What does the man look like?
   3. The suspect is a tall man in his mid twenties. OR Is the suspect a tall man in his mid twenties?
   4. The customer has long, dark hair and big, blue eyes.

⬤⬤⬤
1. police officers	6. police station	11. glad
2. toolbox	7. questions	12. legal
3. tools	8. help	13. rights
4. truth	9. finally	
5. handcuffs	10. angry	

Unit 10: Let the Buyer Beware

Before You Watch (page 128)

- ❂ 2 people arguing   5 photo
-     3 check   6 money
-     4 dessert   1 order pad

- ❂❂ 3 Mr. Brashov and the woman go out to dinner.
-      6 The woman gives Mr. Brashov some money.
-      1 Katherine waits on a new customer.
-      5 Jamal and Katherine show Mr. Brashov a photo.
-      2 The woman and Mr. Brashov argue about the check.
-      4 The waiter hands something to Katherine.

After You Watch (pages 130 and 131)

- ❂ 1. c   2. b   3. c
- ❂❂ 1. f   2. d
- ❂❂❂ 1. a   2. a, e
- ❂ 1. yes   2. yes   3. yes   4. yes

- ❂❂ 2 Barbara tells Mr. Brashov she'll make Crossroads Café famous.
-      4 Mr. Brashov gets his money back.
-      1 Mr. Brashov worries because business is slow.
-      3 Mr. Brashov gives Barbara $800.

- ❂❂❂   Mr. Brashov worries because business is slow. Mr. Brashov and Barbara make a date. Barbara tells Mr. Brashov she will make Crossroads Café famous. Mr. Brashov gives Barbara $800. Jamal takes pictures of Barbara with another man. Barbara sees Jess and Bill hand checks to Mr. Brashov. Mr. Brashov gets his money back.

Your New Language (pages 132 and 133)

- ❂ 1. delicious
-    2. friendly
-    3. wonderful
-    4. smart

- ❂❂ 1. c   2. d   3. b   4. e   5. a

- ❂❂❂ 1. The chef is very skilled.
-      2. The waitstaff works very hard.
-      3. The judges were very generous.

(page 134)

- ❂ 3 Thank you. I'll tell the chef.
-    1 How is everything?
-    2 Fine. The chicken is very good.

- ❂❂ 3 Wow! You must be a very good seamstress.
-     1 I really like your dress.
-     2 Thanks. I made it myself.
-     4 I'm O.K., I guess. Actually, it was pretty easy to make.

ooo _5_ I'm sorry to hear that.

_3_ Really? I thought he was already good.

_7_ Well, I think he's great, too!

_2_ Thank you. He's improved a lot since you became his coach.

_1_ Your son is an excellent baseball player.

_6_ But he is fine now. He thinks you're great.

_4_ Well, he didn't like his last coach, so he didn't do his best for him.

In Your Community (page 135)

o 1. discounted travel and a substantial income

2. $199

3. a free vacation, a lifetime of income, and travel discounts

4. $495

oo 1. to become certified with no test

2. to have a lifetime of income

ooo 1. How much is substantial?

2. How much is the discount?

Read and Write (page 136)

Circle the Answers

o a   oo b   ooo a

Find the Word

o c   oo b   ooo c

Culture Clip (page 139)

o 1. b   2. c   3. a

oo 1. salespeople   5. selling

2. sell   6. businesses

3. careful   7. complain

4. product   8. information

Check Your English (page 140)

o 1. check   3. photo   5. money

2. order pad   4. dessert   6. people arguing

oo 1. This dessert is delicious.

2. You are a trusting man.

3. Crossroads Café is a very charming place.

4. Jamal, you are a very skilled engineer.

ooo 1. worried   6. owner   11. interested

2. date   7. worry   12. money

3. advertise   8. takes   13. sells

4. famous   9. check

5. promote   10. photos

Unit 11: No Vacancy

Before You Watch (page 142)

    ⊙ _3_ excited   _5_ tape measure
         _2_ a big smile   _1_ video camera
         _4_ a person pointing   _6_ videotape

    ⊙⊙ _4_ The apartment manager shows the apartment to a man and a young woman.
      _5_ Jamal measures a room.
      _2_ Rosa looks at an apartment.
      _1_ Jamal helps Henry with a video camera.
      _3_ Rosa receives a phone call.
      _6_ Henry shows the manager his videotape.

After You Watch (pages 144 and 145)

    ⊙ 1. b   2. c   3. e

   ⊙⊙ 1. f   2. d   3. e

  ⊙⊙⊙ 1. a   2. e   3. b

    ⊙ 1. yes   2. no   3. no   4. yes

   ⊙⊙ _3_ The manager tells Rosa the apartment is rented.
      _1_ Rosa wants to move.
      _5_ The Crossroads Café workers decides to prove that Dorothy Walsh discriminated against Rosa.
      _2_ There is an apartment for rent in Katherine's building.
      _4_ Katherine discovers the apartment is not rented.

  ⊙⊙⊙   Rosa can't sleep because of noisy heat and water pipes. Rosa wants to move. There is an apartment for rent in Katheirne's building. The apartment manager offers the apartment to Patty Peterson and her father. The manager tells Rosa the apartment is rented. Katherine finds out the apartment is not rented. The Crossroads Café workers decide to prove the manager has discriminated against Rosa. Rosa decides to file a complaint.

Your New Language (pages 146 and 147)

    ⊙ 1. a little mix up
     2. significant
     3. not settled
     4. not our type

   ⊙⊙ 1. c   2. e   3. a   4. b.   5. d

  ⊙⊙⊙ 1. Do you mean   4. I mean OR That means
     2. you mean   5. Do you mean OR You mean
     3. What do you mean? OR What does that mean?

(page 148)

    ⊙ _2_ JAMAL: Try the button next to the focus control.
      _3_ HENRY: You mean this one?
      _1_ HENRY: Where's the on/off button?

☸☸	2 Jamal:	Discriminate? What exactly does that mean?
	1 Katherine:	Dorothy Walsh is a sweet woman. She would never discriminate against anyone.
	4 Jamal:	You mean, like charge one person more than another for the same thing?
	3 Jess:	It means to treat different people differently.
	5 Jess:	That's right. Or tell someone an apartment is already rented because you don't like the color of his or her skin.

☸☸☸	2 Jess:	A little mix up? That's a bad sign.
	1 Mr. Brashov:	Rosa didn't get the apartment. The manager told her there was a little mix up.
	4 Jess:	I mean I've heard "there's been a little mix up" a lot in my life. It means someone doesn't want her.
	3 Mr. Brashov:	What do you mean, a bad sign?
	5 Mr. Brashov:	You mean Katherine's apartment manager is discriminating against Rosa?
	6 Mr. Brashov:	I'm afraid so.

In Your Community (page 149)

☸ 1. 2 years
2. $600 a month

☸☸ 1. Katherine Blake
2. No. She doesn't have a driver's license

☸☸☸ 1. No. Under proposed occupants she writes N/A.
2. No. Under outstanding balance she wrote zero.

Read and Write (page 150)

Circle the Answers

☸ b   ☸☸ c   ☸☸☸ a

Find the Word

☸ discriminating   ☸☸ reference   ☸☸☸ evict

Culture Clip (page 153)

☸ 1. c   2. a   3. b

☸☸ 1. prejudice   4. reason   7. fear
2. group   5. woman   8. result
3. opinion   6. different   9. laws

Check Your English (page 154)

☸ 1. an excited person   3. videotape   5. a person pointing
2. video camera   4. a big smile   6. tape measure

☸☸ 1. Do you mean this button?
2. What does discrimination mean?
3. Prejudice means deciding without information.
4. Discriminate means to treat people differently.

☸☸☸ 1. building   5. rented   9. lease
2. application   6. discriminating   10. videotape
3. manager   7. rent
4. apartment   8. video camera

Unit 12: Turning Points

Before You Watch (page 156)

- <u>5</u> bruise   <u>1</u> spray paint
- <u>3</u> knife   <u>6</u> gang
- <u>2</u> graffiti   <u>4</u> crime report

- <u>3</u> Mr. Brashov finds a knife.
- <u>1</u> A boy is holding a can of spray paint.
- <u>2</u> The floor is covered with broken glasses and dishes and graffiti is on the walls.
- <u>5</u> A boy has several bruises.
- <u>4</u> The police officer is writing a crime report.
- <u>6</u> Gang members are standing in the café.

After You Watch (pages 158 and 159)

- 1. c   2. d
- 1. d.   2. e
- 1. a.   2. b
- 1. yes   2. no   3. no   4. yes   5. yes

- <u>3</u> Henry recognizes the knife.
- <u>5</u> The police surround the gang members, handcuff them, and take them away.
- <u>1</u> Mr. Brashov arrives one morning and finds that the café has been vandalized.
- <u>2</u> Mr. Brashov sees a knife with Chinese lettering on the wall.
- <u>4</u> Edward tells Henry about the gang.

Mr. Brashov arrives one morning and finds that the café has been vandalized. There is graffiti spray painted on one of the walls. Mr. Brashov sees a knife with Chinese lettering on the wall. Henry recognizes the knife. Edward tells Henry about the gang. Mr. Brashov has a plan to catch the gang. Edward brings the gang to the café to help the police catch the gang. The police surround the gang members, handcuff them, and take them away.

Your New Language (pages 160 and 161)

- 1. in there   3. someday you
- 2. upset   4. beat me up

- 1. e   2. c   3. b   4. d   5. a

- 1. might help   4. might bite
- 2. might   5. might not have
- 3. might think

(page 162)

- <u>1</u> JAMAL: Do you think the gang will come back?
- <u>3</u> JAMAL: Well, we'll be ready for them.
- <u>2</u> MR. BRASHOV: They might come.

- <u>4</u> ROSA: It's the gang's way of telling us that they are strong.
- <u>1</u> ROSA: Look at this knife with Chinese lettering. Who does it belong to?
- <u>3</u> KATHERINE: Why do you think it was on the wall?
- <u>2</u> MR. BRASHOV: It might belong to Henry. He might have left it here when he was opening boxes.

⊙⊙⊙ _5_ JAMAL:	I'd better wait then. I'll check the storeroom for paint. I might need to buy some to cover up the graffiti.
_2_ MR. BRASHOV:	Yes. Actually, we might be closed for a few days.
_4_ MR. BRASHOV:	Be careful not to touch anything. There might be fingerprints.
_3_ JAMAL:	Oh. Well, I'll start to clean up.
_6_ MR. BRASHOV:	Check to see if we have trash bags. You might need to buy some of those, too.
_1_ JAMAL:	Do you want me to make a sign that we will be closed today?

In Your Community (page 163)

⊙ 1. yes   2. yes

⊙⊙ 1. no   2. no

⊙⊙⊙ 1. yes   2. no

Read and Write (page 164)

Circle the Answers

⊙ 1. b   ⊙⊙ 2. a   ⊙⊙⊙ 3. b

Find the Word

⊙ 1. furniture   2. boss

⊙⊙ 1. overturned   2. wrong

⊙⊙⊙ 1. vandalized   2. shattered

Culture Clip (pages 167)

⊙ 1. d
2. c
3. a
4. b

⊙⊙ 1. country	4. gangs	7. programs
2. community	5. skills	8. dangers
3. teach	6. choices	9. differences

Check Your English (page 168)

⊙ 1. bruise	3. spray paint	5. knife
2. crime report	4. gang	6. graffiti

⊙⊙ 1. Do you think the gang might come back?
2. This might make a difference.
3. We might have to close the café for several days.
4. Is there anyone who might be upset with you?

⊙⊙⊙ 1. door	5. vandalized	9. catch
2. graffiti	6. knife	10. surround
3. crime report	7. join	
4. gang	8. bruises	

Unit 13: Trading Places

Before You Watch (page 170)

◌ 1 waiter   5 cook
 3 handyman   2 delivery person
 6 manager   4 busboy

◌◌ 6 Rosa is taking money from a customer at the cash register.
 2 Jamal is delivering the take-out orders.
 1 Henry is waiting on tables.
 3 Mr. Brashov is fixing something at the café.
 5 Katherine is cooking lunch in the kitchen.
 4 Jamal is picking up the dishes from the table.

After You Watch (pages 172 and 173)

◌ 1. d   2. e   3. b   4. c

◌◌ 1. f   2. a

◌◌◌ 1. f   2. b

◌ 1. no, cook   2. yes   3. yes   4. yes   5. no, waiter   6. yes

◌◌ 3 Everyone has a new job. Katherine is cooking; Rosa is giving the customers change; Jamal is delivering take-out orders; and Henry is serving food.
 2 Mr. Brashov plans an experiment to have his employees change jobs for a day.
 1 The employees at Crossroads Café are arguing about whose job is the most important.
 4 It's lunchtime and the regular customers arrive for their meals. There are too many customers.
 5 Customers are yelling for their food and waiting for their change. Take-out orders are late. The experiment is not working.

◌◌◌   The employees at Crossroads Café are arguing about whose job is the most important. Each employee thinks his or her job is the most important. Mr. Brashov plans an experiment and has his employees change jobs for a day. Everyone has a new job. Katherine is cooking; Rosa is bossing people around. Jamal is delivering take-out orders. Henry is serving food. Everyone thinks that the new jobs they are doing are very easy. It's lunchtime and the regular customers arrive for their meals. There are too many customers. The customers are very unhappy. Customers are yelling for their food and waiting for their change. Take-out orders are late. The experiment is not working.

Your New Language (pages 174 and 175)

◌ 1. make
 2. repair
 3. afford
 4. manage

◌◌ 1. e   2. a   3. d   4. c   5. b

◌◌◌ 1. can't   2. can   3. can't   4. don't know how to   5. know how to

(page 176)

◌ 4 KATHERINE: No, I can't, but I can learn.
 2 KATHERINE: Sure. I can make spagetti with meat sauce.
 3 ROSA: Well, can you cook Mexican food?
 1 ROSA: Can you cook Italian food?

⊙⊙	_4_ JAMAL:	Thanks. I'll let you know.
	_2_ JAMAL:	Yes, but I may need some help. I can't do it by myself.
	_3_ MR. BRASHOV:	I can help. Let me know when I can help you.
	_1_ MR. BRASHOV:	There's a leak in the water pipe in the utility room. Do you know how to repair it?
⊙⊙⊙	_5_ MR. BRASHOV:	I don't know. But, Katherine can do that.
	_2_ JESS:	I don't know. Does she know how to work the cash register?
	_3_ MR. BRASHOV:	I think so. But if she doesn't know how to do that, I can teach her.
	_4_ JESS:	Can she place the order for the supplies?
	_1_ MR. BRASHOV:	Do you think Rosa can manage the café?

In Your Community (page 177)

⊙ 1. no   2. yes   3. no   4. yes   5. no   6. yes

⊙⊙ 1. don't know   2. don't know   3. don't know   4. no   5. yes

⊙⊙⊙ 1. yes   2. yes   3. yes   4. no

Read and Write (page 178)

Circle the Answers

⊙ b   ⊙⊙ b   ⊙⊙⊙ a

Find the Word

⊙ a   ⊙⊙ a   ⊙⊙⊙ a

Culture Clip (page 181)

⊙ 1. b   2. c   3. a

⊙⊙ 1. roles   4. rules   7. right
2. marriage   5. couple   8. wrong
3. patterns   6. determine   9. responsibilities

Check Your English (page 182)

⊙ 1. waiter   3. handyman   5. cook
2. delivery person   4. busboy   6. manager

⊙⊙ 1. Rosa can cook a delicious meal. OR Can Rosa cook a delicious meal?
2. Katherine can take orders quickly. OR Can Katherine take orders quickly?
3. Rosa knows how to speak Spanish.
4. Do you know how to speak English?

⊙⊙⊙ 1. job   6. people
2. important   7. delivering
3. experiment   8. serving
4. change   9. lunchtime
5. cooking   10. customers

Student Checklist

UNIT 1

Level	★	★★	★★★
Before You Watch	___ out of 6	___ out of 6	___ out of 6
After You Watch	___ out of 3	___ out of 2	___ out of 1
	___ out of 4	___ out of 4	___ out of 7
Your New Language	___ out of 5	___ out of 5	___ out of 8
	___ out of 4	___ out of 5	___ out of 6
In Your Community	___ out of 3	___ out of 2	___ out of 1
Read and Write	___ out of 1	___ out of 1	___ out of 1
	___ out of 1	___ out of 1	___ out of 1
Culture Clip	___ out of 3	___ out of 7	___ out of 1
Check Your English	___ out of 6	___ out of 4	___ out of 12
TOTAL	___ **out of 36**	___ **out of 37**	___ **out of 44**

UNIT 2

Level	★	★★	★★★
Before You Watch	___ out of 6	___ out of 6	___ out of 6
After You Watch	___ out of 3	___ out of 3	___ out of 2
	___ out of 5	___ out of 6	___ out of 10
Your New Language	___ out of 4	___ out of 5	___ out of 9
	___ out of 4	___ out of 5	___ out of 6
In Your Community	___ out of 2	___ out of 2	___ out of 2
Read and Write	___ out of 1	___ out of 1	___ out of 1
	___ out of 1	___ out of 1	___ out of 1
Culture Clip	___ out of 3	___ out of 7	_____
Check Your English	___ out of 6	___ out of 4	___ out of 10
TOTAL	___ **out of 35**	___ **out of 40**	___ **out of 47**

UNIT 3

Level	⭐	⭐⭐	⭐⭐⭐
Before You Watch	____ out of 6	____ out of 6	____ out of 6
After You Watch	____ out of 3	____ out of 2	____ out of 2
	____ out of 4	____ out of 4	____ out of 7
Your New Language	____ out of 4	____ out of 5	____ out of 8
	____ out of 3	____ out of 5	____ out of 6
In Your Community	____ out of 3	____ out of 2	____ out of 2
Read and Write	____ out of 1	____ out of 1	____ out of 1
	____ out of 1	____ out of 1	____ out of 1
Culture Clip	____ out of 3	____ out of 8	_____
Check Your English	____ out of 6	____ out of 4	____ out of 12
TOTAL	____ **out of 34**	____ **out of 38**	____ **out of 45**

UNIT 4

Level	⭐	⭐⭐	⭐⭐⭐
Before You Watch	____ out of 6	____ out of 6	____ out of 6
After You Watch	____ out of 3	____ out of 2	____ out of 2
	____ out of 4	____ out of 4	____ out of 7
Your New Language	____ out of 4	____ out of 4	____ out of 7
	____ out of 4	____ out of 5	____ out of 7
In Your Community	____ out of 4	____ out of 3	____ out of 2
Read and Write	____ out of 1	____ out of 1	____ out of 1
	____ out of 1	____ out of 1	____ out of 1
Culture Clip	____ out of 4	____ out of 13	_____
Check Your English	____ out of 6	____ out of 4	____ out of 11
TOTAL	____ **out of 37**	____ **out of 43**	____ **out of 44**

UNIT 5

Level	★	★★	★★★
Before You Watch	___ out of 6	___ out of 6	___ out of 6
After You Watch	___ out of 2	___ out of 2	___ out of 1
	___ out of 4	___ out of 5	___ out of 8
Your New Language	___ out of 4	___ out of 5	___ out of 9
	___ out of 3	___ out of 4	___ out of 6
In Your Community	___ out of 2	___ out of 2	___ out of 2
Read and Write	___ out of 1	___ out of 1	___ out of 1
	___ out of 2	___ out of 2	___ out of 2
Culture Clip	___ out of 4	___ out of 8	_____
Check Your English	___ out of 6	___ out of 4	___ out of 10
TOTAL	___ **out of 34**	___ **out of 39**	___ **out of 45**

UNIT 6

Level	★	★★	★★★
Before You Watch	___ out of 6	___ out of 6	___ out of 6
After You Watch	___ out of 2	___ out of 2	___ out of 2
	___ out of 4	___ out of 4	___ out of 7
Your New Language	___ out of 4	___ out of 5	___ out of 4
	___ out of 3	___ out of 5	___ out of 6
In Your Community	___ out of 3	___ out of 3	___ out of 1
Read and Write	___ out of 1	___ out of 1	___ out of 1
	___ out of 1	___ out of 1	___ out of 1
Culture Clip	___ out of 3	___ out of 8	_____
Check Your English	___ out of 6	___ out of 4	___ out of 10
TOTAL	___ **out of 33**	___ **out of 39**	___ **out of 38**

UNIT 7

Level	⭐	⭐⭐	⭐⭐⭐
Before You Watch	____ out of 6	____ out of 6	____ out of 6
After You Watch	____ out of 3	____ out of 2	____ out of 2
	____ out of 4	____ out of 4	____ out of 7
Your New Language	____ out of 4	____ out of 5	____ out of 7
	____ out of 4	____ out of 5	____ out of 6
In Your Community	____ out of 2	____ out of 2	____ out of 2
Read and Write	____ out of 1	____ out of 1	____ out of 1
	____ out of 1	____ out of 1	____ out of 1
Culture Clip	____ out of 4	____ out of 8	_____
Check Your English	____ out of 6	____ out of 4	____ out of 13
TOTAL	____ **out of 35**	____ **out of 38**	____ **out of 45**

UNIT 8

Level	⭐	⭐⭐	⭐⭐⭐
Before You Watch	____ out of 6	____ out of 6	____ out of 6
After You Watch	____ out of 3	____ out of 2	____ out of 2
	____ out of 4	____ out of 4	____ out of 7
Your New Language	____ out of 4	____ out of 5	____ out of 6
	____ out of 3	____ out of 4	____ out of 6
In Your Community	____ out of 2	____ out of 2	____ out of 2
Read and Write	____ out of 1	____ out of 1	____ out of 1
	____ out of 1	____ out of 1	____ out of 1
Culture Clip	____ out of 4	____ out of 8	_____
Check Your English	____ out of 6	____ out of 4	____ out of 12
TOTAL	____ **out of 34**	____ **out of 37**	____ **out of 43**

UNIT 9

Level	★	★★	★★★
Before You Watch	___ out of 6	___ out of 6	___ out of 6
After You Watch	___ out of 3	___ out of 3	___ out of 2
	___ out of 4	___ out of 4	___ out of 7
Your New Language	___ out of 5	___ out of 5	___ out of 8
	___ out of 4	___ out of 6	___ out of 7
In Your Community	___ out of 4	___ out of 2	___ out of 2
Read and Write	___ out of 1	___ out of 1	___ out of 1
	___ out of 1	___ out of 1	___ out of 1
Culture Clip	___ out of 3	___ out of 11	_____
Check Your English	___ out of 6	___ out of 4	___ out of 13
TOTAL	___ **out of 37**	___ **out of 43**	___ **out of 47**

UNIT 10

Level	★	★★	★★★
Before You Watch	___ out of 6	___ out of 6	___ out of 6
After You Watch	___ out of 3	___ out of 2	___ out of 2
	___ out of 4	___ out of 4	___ out of 7
Your New Language	___ out of 4	___ out of 5	___ out of 3
	___ out of 3	___ out of 4	___ out of 7
In Your Community	___ out of 4	___ out of 2	___ out of 2
Read and Write	___ out of 1	___ out of 1	___ out of 1
	___ out of 1	___ out of 1	___ out of 1
Culture Clip	___ out of 3	___ out of 8	_____
Check Your English	___ out of 6	___ out of 4	___ out of 13
TOTAL	___ **out of 35**	___ **out of 37**	___ **out of 42**

Unit 11

Level	★	★★	★★★
Before You Watch	___ out of 6	___ out of 6	___ out of 6
After You Watch	___ out of 3	___ out of 3	___ out of 3
	___ out of 4	___ out of 5	___ out of 8
Your New Language	___ out of 4	___ out of 5	___ out of 5
	___ out of 3	___ out of 5	___ out of 6
In Your Community	___ out of 2	___ out of 2	___ out of 2
Read and Write	___ out of 1	___ out of 1	___ out of 1
	___ out of 1	___ out of 1	___ out of 1
Culture Clip	___ out of 3	___ out of 9	_____
Check Your English	___ out of 6	___ out of 4	___ out of 10
TOTAL	___ **out of 33**	___ **out of 41**	___ **out of 42**

Unit 12

Level	★	★★	★★★
Before You Watch	___ out of 6	___ out of 6	___ out of 6
After You Watch	___ out of 2	___ out of 2	___ out of 2
	___ out of 5	___ out of 5	___ out of 8
Your New Language	___ out of 4	___ out of 5	___ out of 5
	___ out of 3	___ out of 4	___ out of 6
In Your Community	___ out of 2	___ out of 2	___ out of 2
Read and Write	___ out of 1	___ out of 1	___ out of 1
	___ out of 2	___ out of 2	___ out of 2
Culture Clip	___ out of 4	___ out of 9	_____
Check Your English	___ out of 6	___ out of 4	___ out of 10
TOTAL	___ **out of 35**	___ **out of 40**	___ **out of 42**

Unit 13

Level	★	★★	★★★
Before You Watch	____ out of 6	____ out of 6	____ out of 6
After You Watch	____ out of 4	____ out of 2	____ out of 2
	____ out of 6	____ out of 5	____ out of 8
Your New Language	____ out of 4	____ out of 5	____ out of 5
	____ out of 4	____ out of 4	____ out of 5
In Your Community	____ out of 5	____ out of 6	____ out of 4
Read and Write	____ out of 1	____ out of 1	____ out of 1
	____ out of 1	____ out of 1	____ out of 1
Culture Clip	____ out of 3	____ out of 9	_____
Check Your English	____ out of 6	____ out of 4	____ out of 10
TOTAL	____ **out of 40**	____ **out of 43**	____ **out of 42**

Index

V

vandalized, 164
vegetarian, 52
video camera, 143
videotape, 143
violin, 17

W

waiter, 171
wallet, 87
watch, 73
wires, 45
work-study form, 17
wrong, 164